HEADLINE: STARKWEATHER

Published 1993 by Journal-Star Printing Co.

Murderer's own story is reprinted with permission from Parade magazine, copyright © 1959.

Library of Congress Cataloging-in-Publication Data

HEADLINE: STARKWEATHER/Earl Dyer

p.   cm.
ISBN 0-933909-08-X
1. Starkweather, Charles. 2. Fugate, Caril. 3. Murder — Nebraska. 4. History — Nebraska. 5. Crime and the Press. 6. Capital Punishment. 7. Crime — Mass Murder. I. Dyer, Earl. II. Title.
1993   93-77608
First Edition

Printed in the United States of America
by
Cornhusker Press   Hastings, Nebraska

Cover design by Brian Noonan

HEADLINE: STARKWEATHER

From behind the news desk.

by Earl Dyer

Foreword

Thirty-five years ago, a pair of teen-agers killed nine people in the Lincoln, Neb., area, causing panic in the city and across the state and creating a national news story that remains alive even today. Criticism of how police handled the case resulted in a formal investigation. And the series of events set off a period of community introspection about services for troubled young people.

But the story didn't end when Charles Starkweather was executed 17 months later, or when Caril Fugate was released from parole Sept. 28, 1981.

Throughout the 35 years since the murders there have been books, magazine articles, television shows, a movie and at least one song by a popular singer about the dramatic events. A new TV miniseries is scheduled for national network presentation at about the time this book is to be published. An important source of information for all of these projects has been the news clipping files of the Journal-Star Printing Co., which continues to get at least one request every month for information about the Starkweather murderers, librarian Pat Loos estimates.

The Starkweather files, covering the period from the day the first bodies were found (Jan. 27, 1958) through the commutation of Caril Fugate's sentence (Oct. 31, 1973), have been pasted into a 146-page newspaper-size scrapbook. In reporting those stories to their readers (about 25,000 subscribers then for The Star in the morning, about 44,600 for the Lincoln Evening Journal), the Lincoln newspapers used more than 70 tons of newsprint. At the time, the newspapers carried eight columns of type on each page, and there were perhaps 1,100 columns devoted to the Starkweather story. The number of words is hard to calculate — part of that space was taken up with pictures and headlines — but a reasonable estimate might be 750,000 words.

My attempt in this book has been to let the reporters, photographers and editors of The Lincoln Star and the Lincoln Journal of those days tell the story — they are the real authors of this book. Their headlines and stories capture the drama of the times in a way that cannot be duplicated. Those headlines and stories also illustrate the underlying imperfections of the newspaper business of the day; deadlines had to be met, meaning there often was little chance to check information and even less chance to be sure the stories were well written.

Throughout this book, the material set full width and in sans serif type is mine; passages set in serif type and indented are direct quotations from the newspapers. In many cases the stories are repeated here in shortened form, to avoid repetition. Because many of the stories were being handled on deadline with no chance to proofread the type, there were a substantial number of typographical errors, which have been corrected here in the interest of clarity.

This book is intended to show how the two hometown papers covered these world-famous news events, and by inference it shows the information on which the public made its judgments about the case. This book is in no way intended to be a complete investigation of the Starkweather case. One such attempt has been published — *Starkweather, The Story of a Mass Murderer,* by William Allen, published in 1976. A criminology text by University of Nebraska professor James M. Reinhardt, *The Murderous Trail of Charles Starkweather,* was published in 1960. *Caril,* by Ninette Beaver, B.K. Ripley and Patrick Trese, was published in 1974 (to a scathing review by a reporter who had followed the case closely).

This book is based in part on my own memory of the events and how the newspapers reported them at the time. I am indebted to Neale Copple, former city editor of the Journal (now retired dean of the University of Nebraska College of Journalism), and to Marj Marlette, retired Journal reporter, for sharing the observations credited to them.

The photographs used here — from the Journal-Star's own files — are the work of Bob Gorham, Willis Van Sickle, Bob McKay, Frank O'Neill and Web Ray. The courtroom sketches were done by Sally Raglin.

Steve Batie planned and executed the layout of the book and Linda Olig assisted with editing; both made invaluable suggestions.

Most of all, I am indebted to the reporters who, in writing these stories, caught so vividly the drama of those times.

— Earl Dyer
February 1993

Contents

Each day, 3 more bodies

A QUIET DAY EXPLODES

Jan. 27, 1958.

Lincoln, Nebraska, a small (pop. 128,000) state capital, seat of the state university; home of two newspapers: The Lincoln Star, morning; the Lincoln Evening Journal, evening.

The weather was typical for January: high temperature 29, snow forecast for later in the week.

City editor Earl Dyer arrived a bit before 4 p.m. at his desk in The Star newsroom on the second floor of the Journal-Star Building and began going over the news so far that day, as well as early accounts from reporters of what might be expected for the next morning's paper. The first edition was to go to press at 7:45 p.m.

Dyer took his seat at the center (called the "slot") of a large desk that had arranged around it the desks of wire editors and other copy editors. Reporters' desks faced the slot. The few windows were narrow and horizontal, admitting little daylight. It was a noisy newsroom — typewriters made much more sound than the computer terminals that have replaced them; clattering teletype machines brought in wire service reports; a loudspeaker announced Associated Press wirephoto transmissions; nearby, a squawking police radio carried police broadcasts to cruisers.

The central news desk was a sea of paper — the long ribbons from the teletypes, stories from reporters, copies of newspapers fresh from the press, page layouts and assignment sheets. Cigarette burns lined the edges of the desks.

The day's news didn't look exciting.

Big stories included an education program outlined by President Dwight D. Eisenhower and refusal by Nebraska Gov. Victor Anderson to call a special session of the Legislature on taxes, as sought by a prominent state senator.

The sports section would carry a big headline that the Western Baseball League (Lincoln's team was affiliated with the Pittsburgh major league team) might have eight teams the next summer. On the women's pages there would be reports of social affairs, club meetings, one marriage engagement and the Dear Abby column (in those days edited by the managing editor to remove any potentially salacious content). Locally, the Unitarian Church was kicking off a fund drive to build a new church, and on the editorial page it would be noted that the national debt was pushing $280 billion — but that the man on the street would little note the effect.

The routine nature of the day was not to last long.

Shortly after 4:30 p.m., the police radio began to crackle. Authorities, summoned by relatives, had found three bodies in the outbuildings of a small, ramshackle residence in a poor section of town.

It was a huge story.

Though he carried his own big, heavy Speedgraphic camera, police reporter Del Harding called for help from photographers. Staff members began the frantic search for information about the victims and for pictures of them.

Harding's story in the next morning's Star appeared under a big, black, eight-column headline — hand set in 120-point type (one and a half inches high) — all in capital letters.

His story read:

> Three members of the Marion Bartlett family — apparently the victims of a triple murder — were found dead about 4:30 p.m. Monday in two sheds behind their home at 924 Belmont.
>
> Dead are: Marion Bartlett, 57; his wife, Velda, 37; and their daughter, Betty Jean, who would have been 3 on Feb. 11th.
>
> County Attorney Elmer Scheele said a preliminary autopsy report showed the parents died as the result of small-caliber bullet wounds in the head. There were also cuts "about their bodies" which "may have been made by a knife," Scheele said.
>
> The little girl apparently died of a skull fracture, it was reported. There were no bullet wounds.
>
> Scheele said no one has been taken into custody in connection with the crime, but added authorities are seeking Mrs. Bartlett's daughter by a previous marriage and her boyfriend for questioning. He identified them as Caril Fugate, 15, and Charles R. Starkweather, 19.
>
> The girl reportedly lived with her mother and step-father at 924 Belmont. A positive address on Starkweather was not available (but he is a Lincoln resident).
>
> Police in six states are seeking the pair, who reportedly were last seen about 5:30 p.m. Monday southbound from Lincoln. Scheele said they "may be armed" but declined to elaborate.
>
> Authorities reported the bodies of the Bartletts were found by

NEBRASKA Considerable cloudiness with no important temperature changes Tuesday and Tuesday night; high Tuesday around 30 extreme east and 40 to 45 west.

THE LINCOLN STAR

Fire 2-2222   Telephone 2-1234   Police 2-2841

FIFTY-SIXTH YEAR   No. 102   LINCOLN, NEB., TUESDAY MORNING, JANUARY 28, 1958   SEVEN CENTS

BELMONT FAMILY SLAIN

★ ★ ★ ★ ★ ★ ★ ★

—Congress—

Atomic Gifts Asked

T_ _er Is Urged To Give Allies A-Secrets

WASHINGTON (AP)— The Eisenhower administration asked Congress Monday for authority to give U.S. allies hitherto secret atomic weapons information, as well as raw materials and weapon components.

The Atomic Energy Commission (AEC) offered proposed legislation to carry out the President's recommendations for backing up the free world's atomic defenses and avoiding duplication of atomic work among allies.

AEC chairman Lewis L. Strauss proposed that the President be given discretion to exchange any atomic weapon information with an ally which is making "substantial and material contributions to the national defense and security."

The authorizations provided by AECs proposed amendments to the Atomic Energy Act would stop short of providing for transfer of complete atomic weapons to other countries.

Strauss said "it is not the intent . . . to promote the export of additional nations into the atomic weapons field." The proposed legislation is worded to encourage "exchanges" of information with nations already active in the field — presumably Britain and possibly Canada and France.

Hearings

Rep. Durham (D-NC), chairman of the Senate-House Atomic Energy Committee and Sen. Pastore (D-RI), chairman of its subcommittee on international agreements, said the legislative proposals were referred to in his committee and will be considered at executive sessions Wednesday, Thursday and Friday. Pastore arranges will be held later, they added.

Eisenhower emphasized in his message that the main purpose of the proposed legislation or removing restrictions on exchange of scientific and technical information with friendly countries. He said this would mean that all the efforts of the free world could be mobilized to stay ahead of the Soviet bloc in technological war readiness.

The proposed amendments would remove from the act prohibitions against revealing "important information concerning the design or fabrication of the nuclear components of an atomic weapon." All so defined would be a ban against furnishing special nuclear material in amount sufficient for military purposes.

The law as AEC proposed to have it amended would authorize non-nuclear parts of atomic weapons, military reactors and nuclear materials to be furnished to allies. Nuclear components of U.S. weapons would be retained in U.S. custody.

The Weather

[weather data table]

Authorities eye scene where bodies found. Two bodies were found in the shed at the left and one in the shed at right. The box in which one of the victims was located is in front of investigators. (Star Photo).

Navy Try At Space Given Up

Army Effort To Orbit Satellite Said Near

CAPE CANAVERAL, Fla. (AP)— An attempt to launch the Army's Jupiter-C earth satellite appeared near Monday night.

The Navy plainly has deferred its own try in the Vanguard rocket and the Army effort once more has cleared the air . . . once again Tuesday and next were scheduled.

Unusual activity around the heavy launching area — apparatus in the interview of large cranes and other vehicles — could be observed from vantage point the closely guarded missile test center.

Furthermore, personnel discarded with the project have frightened new earlier questions of spaces items.

Dismantled

Indications of renewed Army preparations for a Jupiter-C launch attempt this week or next coincided with the partial dismantling of the Navy's Vanguard satellite bearing rocket. The Navy was observed removing the second stage of its 72-foot rocket, obviously for corrective work.

Watchers guessed that there was little doubt that the Navy had given up for the present its effort to try a 3-inch satellite into orbit, and then had left the field wide open for the Army Jupiter-C effort.

This new developments in the milesterone-dogged Vanguard program became evident only because, after days of rain and fog the launching towers on the case again were highly visible in bright sunlight.

Secrecy

Secrecy cloaking plans for the two satellite projects remained as strict as ever. The Defense Department and the various services assigned to the programs are trying hard to prevent a buildup of the pressures and tensions of which surrounded the Dec. 6 Vanguard launch attempt.

In that earlier try, the chances of success were badly exaggerated. The result was disappointment and unsettled for bitterness when the Vanguard blew up on its launching pad.

The Navy tried valiantly, much of last week to get its complex test vehicle through the last stages of its pre-launching program.

Heavy rains and high winds day after day, compounded their problems, as did a series of mechanical

The Bartlett home—only a puppy there.

Tax Committee Has Spent $1,467

...Terry's Group Expenses Largest

By BETTY PERSON
Star Staff Writer

Sen. Otto Liebers of Lincoln, chairman of the executive committee of the Legislative Council, Monday released to the press figures showing expenditures of each legislative committee, with the Tax Law Violations Committee heading the list with expenses of $1,467.

Liebers said last Friday following a meeting of the executive committee. One resolution has a committee room in the state of . . .

U.S. Lags In Arms To Troops

...Says Quarles

WASHINGTON (P)—Deputy Secretary of Defense Donald A. Quarles has told senators the chances of keeping military equipment for the ground forces.

Quarles testimony, taken behind closed doors by the Senate's Preparedness subcommittee and just now released indicated a new field in which the United States may be lagging behind Russia.

The subcommittee previously had heard statements of a few Generals and other military and range missiles and satellite development.

Questioned by Edwin L. Weisl, subcommittee counsel about Russian ground power of what he called Tempo's artillery, Quarles said the Soviets have always been 'very advanced' in equipping their ground forces.

'concede'

"I think that in detail one might dispute some of these advantages."

Stay away Every Body Is Sick With The Flu. Miss Bartlett

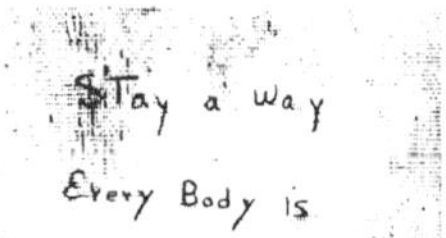

This note was left on the door.

New Red Talk Offer Is Issued

...By Khrushchev

MOSCOW (P)—N.S. Khrushchev Monday proposed a summit conference at which the East and West could work with simple problems and work up to the tougher ones.

The Soviet Communist party chief said such a conference could begin with power, he can agree on before tackling the tougher and more basic problems that divide the East and West.

Khrushchev made his proposal before the latest in a series of Soviet calls for a summit conference to a group of western governors at an Indian National Day Reception.

8 CLUBS IN WL IN '58?

Colorado Springs is making a determined bid to re-enter the Western League in 1958, and Sioux City also is reported ready to re-apply in the loop which is now a six-team circuit.

Both clubs recently dropped out of the Western League. See Sports Editor Don Bryant's story on Sports Page 11.

Partly Cloudy Skies Forecast

Considerably cloudy skies with high readings of 30 in the east and all to 45 in the west were predicted

Tot And Parents Found Dead In Apparent Murder

Daughter, Boyfriend Sought For Questioning; Couple Shot, Child Had Skull Fracture

By DEL HARDING
Star Staff Writer

Three members of the Marion Bartlett family apparently the victims of a triple murder — were found dead about 4:00 p.m. Monday in two sheds behind their home at 924 Belmont.

Dead are Marion Bartlett, 57; his wife, Velda, 37, and their daughter, Betty Jean, who would have been 3 on Feb. 11th.

County Attorney Elmer Scheele said a prominent weapon shooting of the parents shed as the result of small caliber wounds in the head. There were also indications that they were shot about five years made by a knife. Scheele said the little girl apparently died of a skull fracture; it was reported.

There were no bullet wounds.

Scheele said no one has been taken into custody in connection with the crime, but added authorities are seeking one Bartlett daughter, Caril Ann, 14, and her boyfriend, Charles "Chuck" Starkweather, 19.

Authorities reported the bodies of the Bartletts were found by Robert Von Busch, 20, son-in-law of Mrs. Bartlett and Rodney Starkweather, 21, brother of Charles.

Von Busch and Rodney Stark weather had reportedly gone to the house to see if anything was wrong after Mrs. Bartlett's mother—Mrs. Pansey Street of Lincoln had been refused admittance to the house about 3 p.m. Monday.

By Carrol Fugate

Mrs. Street reportedly then returned to the home about 10 a.m. with two police detectives, but found a note tied over the police escorted the two away from the door and finding indignantly wrong since this. The girl said the note read stay away, every body is sick with the flu.

Bartlett's family was both wrapped in rags and discarded muffs in a chicken coop and the bodies of Mrs. Bartlett and young Betty Jean were found in an abandoned outhouse. Scheele said the bodies were not dismembered.

A head-written sign on the home's front door had stayed wrong "Stay a way Every Body is sick with the flue." It was signed "Miss Bartlett."

Aberal For Week

Frank McKay, manager of Watson Bros. Lincoln office where Bartlett was employed, said Bartlett had been to work for more than a week. "Someone had called in and reported him sick," he added, "and Bartlett had no phone so nobody called him to see what happened."

The county attorney said it had not yet been determined how long the Bartletta had been dead before their bodies were found.

The car Charles Starkweather reportedly was driving was described as a 1949 black Ford, 1957 license number 2-1958. The car has its grille missing and has no package, police said.

The slayings recall the recent unsolved murder of Robert Colvert of Lincoln, 21-year-old service station attendant also shot in the head.

He died from a shotgun blast early the morning of Dec. 1. After reportedly being robbed of more than $100 in a holdup at the Crest Service Station at 1548 Cornhusker—which is only about a mile from the Bartlett home.

Bartlett   Mrs. Bartlett   Betty Jean

U.S., Russ OK Plan On Swaps

...2-Year Exchange

WASHINGTON (P)—The United States and Russia Monday agreed on a momentous two-year swap of films, radio-television broadcasts and about 300 students in everything from ballet dancing to horse doctoring.

Deputy Under Secretary of State William S.B. Lacy and Soviet Ambassador Georgi Zaroubin called it the most important achievement of his five years in Washington.

President Eisenhower applauded the accord, saying he hoped it would be carried out in the same spirit which has animated the negotiations.

WASHINGTON (P)—The United States and Russia Monday agreed such agreements a better understanding will result through several goodwill result between the peoples of the United States and the Soviet Union.

Hailed

The State Department issued a statement hailing the agreement as a "significant first step in the improvement of mutual understanding."

The department, mirroring Eisenhower's words, declared:

"It is a sincerely hoped that it will be carried out in such a way as to contribute substantially to the betterment of relations between the two countries, thereby also contributing to a lessening of international tensions."

Conspicuously absent from the agreement were the two things the United States most wanted: An end to Kremlin jamming of Voice of America Russian language broadcasts to the Soviet Union, and regular unmonitored radio-TV commentaries on world events.

Strike Is Staged By 275 Inmates At Montana Pen

DEER LODGE, Mont. (P)—About 275 inmates of the Montana State Prison staged a sudden strike Monday. Warden F. O. Burrell said there was no violence.

It was the first reported disturbance at the institution since a violent riot last July 30 in which several guards were held for a while as hostage.

Burrell said Monday night he did not know what caused the disorder.

The warden said the strikers represent less than half the number of prisoners in the institution. The population is 604, he said.

The prisoners began their demonstration quietly and without warning shortly after breakfast.

The warden said they reported for work and as the protest and then the ringleaders apparently passed the word.

Armed guards herded the strikers behind bars in the maximum security cellblock without difficulty.

Burrell said. However, the strikers refused efforts to make them return to their individual cells at night.

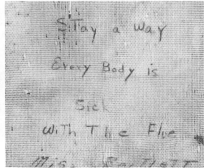

LEFT and BELOW: The first bodies were found near a ramshackle house in the Belmont neighborhood. **ABOVE:** A note (enhanced by the papers to improve reproduction) on the front door warned away visitors.

Robert Von Busch, 19 (a son-in-law of Mrs. Bartlett), and Rodney Starkweather, 21, brother of Charles.

Von Busch and Rodney Starkweather had reportedly gone to see if anything was wrong after Mrs. Bartlett's mother — Mrs. Pansey Street of Lincoln — had been refused admittance to the home about 9 a.m. Monday by Caril Fugate.

Mrs. Street reportedly then returned to the home about 10 a.m. with two police detectives, but found Caril had gone. The police entered the home through a window and, finding nothing apparently wrong, they left. They did not check the two sheds at the rear of the house, which later yielded the bodies.

Bartlett's body was found wrapped in rags and discarded quilts in a chicken house and the bodies of Mrs. Bartlett and young Betty Jean were found in an abandoned outhouse. Scheele said the bodies were not dismembered.

A hand-written sign on the home's front door had this warning: "Stay a Way. Every Body is Sick With The Flue." It was signed "Miss Bartlett."

Frank McKay, manager of Watson Bros. Lincoln office, where Bartlett was employed, said Bartlett had not been to work for more than a week. "Someone had called in and reported him sick," he added, "and Bartlett had no phone so nobody called him to see what happened."

The county attorney said it had not yet been determined how long the Bartletts had been dead before their bodies were found.

The car Charles Starkweather reportedly was driving was described as a 1949 black Ford, 1957 license number 2-15628. The car has its grille missing and has no hubcaps, police said.

The slayings recall the recent murder of Robert Colvert of Lincoln, 21-year-old service station attendant also shot in the head.

He died from a shotgun blast early the morning of Dec. 1, after apparently being robbed at the Crest Service Station at 1545 Cornhusker — which is only about a mile from the Bartlett home.

— *Star, Jan. 28, 1958*

All editions of The Star that night went to press on time. Luckily, the bodies had been found well before the first Star presstime — 7:45 p.m. During the rest of the week, Star staffers continued to meet their deadlines, because all the main developments occurred during daytime hours, but stories were updated constantly with additional details during edition changes through each of the nights. And reporters worked long hours rounding up details for the many developing stories.

The Journal was not to be so lucky about meeting deadlines.

THREE MORE BODIES

On the other side of the wall separating Star and Journal newsrooms, Journal staff members worked in surroundings similar to those in the Star, except that their office was in the middle of the building and had no windows. There were the same clattering teletypes and typewriters, noisy loudspeakers, a semi-circular "slot" desk — but with the city editor's desk off to one side facing reporter desks — and all of it swimming in a sea of paper.

Journal city editor Neale Copple and some of his staff had spent much of the night on what would come to be called the Starkweather story. They'd been able to nail down information not available to Star reporters the previous night, and in a kind of coup in Lincoln's competitive newspaper market, one Journal reporter visiting the scene of the crime had been able to pocket a photo of Charles Starkweather and Caril Fugate, the two young people being sought for questioning in the murders. A zinc plate for reprinting the photo was quickly produced in the Journal-Star plant and the picture returned.

The Star's story had been updated with new information through edition changes the night before, and Copple envisioned his task as much the same. A manhunt continued for the two missing teen-agers, and there was growing suspicion they were connected with the Colvert murder several weeks earlier.

The Journal's first edition (press time: 9 a.m.) rounded up the facts under a headline that said:

Two Sought for Questioning In Belmont Triple Slaying

The story, under the byline of Journal police reporter Del Snodgrass, quoted law enforcement officers still cautiously saying that Charles Starkweather and Caril Fugate were wanted "for what light they might shed on the case." Snodgrass' story carried the results of a preliminary autopsy and more generous background on the victims and the scene of the crime:

> A 15-year-old girl and her 19-year-old companion were being sought Tuesday for questioning in connection with the apparent murder of a Lincoln couple and their two-year-old child.
>
> Police broadcast a general alarm for Caril Fugate, a daughter of the dead woman, and Charles R. Starkweather, whose address police gave as 3025 N.
>
> Police Chief Joe Carroll said the two young persons were wanted "for what light they might shed on the case."
>
> Lancaster Co. Att. Elmer Scheele identified the three dead Lincolnites as Marion Bartlett, 57; his wife, Velda, 37; and their daughter, Betty Jean, who would have been three on Feb. 11.
>
> Bartlett and his wife, their bodies wrapped in paper and rags,

This photo, taken by a Journal reporter from the Bartlett murder scene, was the first published of Charles Starkweather and Caril Fugate.

and the child, her body in a cardboard box, were discovered late Monday afternoon in rickety outbuildings behind their home at 924 Belmont in North Lincoln.

Scheele said a preliminary autopsy showed both Bartletts were shot in the head "with a small caliber weapon," and had lacerations, apparently stab wounds, about their bodies.

The child died of skull fractures and lacerations but apparently had not been shot, he said.

Authorities said the time of death probably would not be known for several days until further examinations are completed.

The Fugate girl, Scheele continued, is the daughter of Mrs. Bartlett by a previous marriage. He said she and Starkweather were believed together driving a 1949 black Ford, its grille broken out, hubcaps missing and bearing Nebraska license 2-15628.

It was believed the pair might be headed south for Kansas.

Scheele said Caril lived with her mother and stepfather at the Belmont address where the bodies were found. According to County Court records the Bartletts were married in 1954.

Investigating officials gave this sequence of Monday's events which led up to the discovery of the bodies.

Mrs. Bartlett's mother, Mrs. Pansy Street of 425 No. 10th, went to the Bartlett home at approximately 9 a.m. but was refused entrance to the house by Caril Fugate.

Mrs. Street became suspicious and contacted police. Two detectives went to the house, found no one home, entered through a window but found nothing amiss.

At approximately 4 p.m., Robert Von Busch of 425 No. 10th and Charles' brother, Rodney Starkweather of 1118 H, went to the house and checked the outbuildings, where they discovered two of the bodies.

Police were notified and went to the scene. Bartlett's body, wrapped in paper, was found in a small chicken coop a short distance behind the house.

Mrs. Bartlett's body was found wrapped in what appeared to be old bed clothing and the baby's body was in a cardboard box. Both were located a few feet west of the chicken coop.

Von Busch's wife, Barbara, is the dead woman's daughter by the previous marriage.

According to authorities, several relatives of the Bartletts had been to the house recently but were told by Caril that the entire family was ill with the flu.

A handwritten note was found on the front door of the home Monday. It read: "Stay a Way, Every Body is Sick With The Flue (sic)." It was signed "Miss Bartlett."

Although Police Chief Carroll said the inside of the Bartlett home showed no "immediate" signs of a struggle, he said the house was littered and unkept.

The house is covered with colored tar paper and a board walk leads over a dirt yard from the street to the front door.

A small puppy was found inside the house and an older, larger dog outside.

Bartlett was a night watchman for the Watson Bros. trucking firm offices in Lincoln. Frank McKay, local Watson manager, said his office had a received a call from some person about a week ago saying Mr. Bartlett was ill and would not report for work.

Chief Carroll said Charles Starkweather, the youth sought with Caril Fugate for questioning, had been a garbage truck driver and had worked with his brother, Rodney, 21.

Autopsies on the three bodies were performed at Lincoln General Hospital by Dr. Frank H. Tanner, Lincoln pathologist.

— *Journal, Jan. 28, 1958*

In the terminology of the newsroom, that story was not to "stand" very long. The Journal's editions that day carried six different banner headlines and stories that were expanded in each edition — sometimes in mid-edition. So frequent were the changes — and so close to deadlines as the day wore on — that Journal news editor Gilbert Savery listened in on Copple's conversations with reporters and was writing headlines even before the stories themselves could be completed.

The first and subsequent editions of the Journal also carried a brief story about the possible connection with the earlier murder:

Colvert Case Is Recalled

The deaths of a Lincoln couple and their child recalled the unsolved, nearly two-month-old Robert Colvert murder case.

Colvert, a night attendant at the Crest Service Station on Cornhusker Highway, apparently was robbed at the station early Dec. 1, then driven to a county road north of Lincoln where he was shot in the head with a shotgun.

So far authorities have failed to solve the case.

— *Journal, Jan. 28, 1958*

All editions of the Journal that day carried across the top of the page this story about the discovery of the bodies:

Events Leading to Grim Discovery
Recounted by Bartlett Relatives

Last Tuesday was the last time that Mrs. Barbara Von Busch, 17, saw her mother, Mrs. Marion Bartlett, one of the apparent murder victims at 924 Belmont.

The events that followed increasingly disturbed Barbara, her husband, Robert, 18, and Mrs. Pansy Street, all of 425 No. 10th. Mrs.

Street is the mother of Mrs. Marion Bartlett.

Here is the sequence of those events as described by the Von Busches and Mrs. Street:

Tuesday (Jan. 21): Mrs. Von Busch said that Mrs. Bartlett told her that she had some film and that she would bring the pictures when they had been developed.

Charles Starkweather and Caril Fugate, the missing young couple, went to the home of Harvey Griggs of 1179 Furnas where Starkweather left his car and the keys.

About the same time, Bartlett, 57-year-old night watchman for Watson Bros. trucking firm offices in Lincoln, was reported sick by some person saying Bartlett would not report for work.

Company officials said they heard nothing further from the employee.

About Thursday: Mrs. Von Busch says she was told by a friend of the family that the friend had gone to the Bartletts to buy eggs and was turned away.

Mrs. Von Busch said she also heard that the owner of the Bartlett home was turned away by Caril.

Neighbors of the Bartletts said it was generally known in the neighborhood that Bartlett was in the process of buying the Belmont residence from the owner.

Saturday: The Von Busches went to the Bartlett residence and were met by Caril, who told them both the Bartletts and their two-year-old daughter were sick with the "five-day flu" and no one was allowed to see them.

Robert Von Busch became alarmed at the 14-year-old's statement and notified Lincoln police.

9:30 p.m. Saturday: According to police officials, two police officers were sent to 924 Belmont and also were met at the door by Caril who told officers no one was allowed in the house due to "doctor's orders."

Monday, 9 a.m.: Mrs. Pansy Street took a cab at about 9 a.m. because she says she was worried about her daughter's unexplained illness. Mrs. Street was turned away by Caril.

Mrs. Street said she pleaded with the granddaughter to permit her to at least talk with the family through the door and when she received no satisfaction, Mrs. Street said she called for two-year-old Betty Jean "to speak to Granny."

Mrs. Street said, "I headed back downtown and told police that something was wrong."

9:30 to 10 a.m. Monday: Two detectives were sent to the Belmont residence and were unable to arouse anyone. They entered the house through the window and reported finding nothing amiss.

About 3:30 p.m. Monday: Robert Von Busch drove to the Bartlett home and found that no one was home. He then drove to police headquarters and requested officials to investigate.

Von Busch said police officials told him that the Bartletts had probably gone on vacation.

Von Busch drove back to the Bartlett residence with Rodney Starkweather of 1118 H, a brother of the missing youth, and found the house still empty and in checking the outbuildings discovered two of the bodies. The third was found later.

— Journal, Jan. 28, 1958

The next Journal version of the main story (press time 1:30 p.m.) carried the headline:

Bartletts   Were   Dead
Two Days When Found

Immediately below that, a "lead-all" in boldface (a paragraph hurriedly placed at the top of a story to relate late developments) moved the scene of the action out of Lincoln: "Officials were converging on a farmhouse near Bennet, where it was thought the two teen-agers sought for questioning in the triple slaying might be."

Inserted into the story was a boldface paragraph reporting: "The county sheriff's office reported that Carol King, 16, and Robert Jensen, 17, who live in the Bennet area, have been missing overnight. Officers said that young Jensen had picked the King girl up at 6 p.m. Monday and they had not returned."

With those two terse bulletins, the story reported:

A 1949 model automobile believed to have been used by two teenagers wanted for questioning in connection with an apparent triple murder in Lincoln has been located east of Bennet, the Nebraska Safety Patrol said shortly after noon.

The patrol said the car was apparently abandoned about 1½ miles east of the Lancaster County maintenance shops at Bennet.

No one was found near the automobile.

As the search for the two youths broadened into other states, these were other developments in the investigation of the apparent triple murder:

1. It was reported that the victims had been dead "at least" 48 hours before their bodies were found.

2. Law enforcement officers were combing the house at 924 Belmont for clues.

Police broadcast a general alarm for Caril Fugate, 15, a daughter of the dead woman, and Charles R. Starkweather, 19, whose address police gave as 2025 N.

— Journal, Jan. 28, 1958

The next Journal headline (at 2:50 p.m.) read:

Search for Teenagers Is Centered on Bennet

That story reported:

Twenty law enforcement officers began surrounding the August Meyer farm home two miles east of Bennet Tuesday afternoon in search of two Lincoln teenagers wanted in connection with an apparent triple murder.

Officials began the maneuver in the belief that the youths may be at the home occupied by the elderly bachelor farmer.

Some person or persons answered the telephone calls placed to the home by the Journal but hung up the phone without making any statements.

The Lancaster County Sheriff's Office said officials from that office, Lincoln city police and the Nebraska State Patrol were surrounding the farmstead. In addition, more than 30 local residents had gathered at the scene.

A request was made by the officials at the scene for a loudspeaker unit to be brought from Lincoln.

Officers began surrounding the home after Pat Boldt, a Bennet garageman, and Safety Patrolman Vernon R. O'Neal of Lincoln spotted a black 1949 or 1950 model automobile in Meyer's driveway.

The auto was believed to have been one occupied by Caril Fugate, 14, a daughter of the dead Lincoln woman, and Charles R. Starkweather, 19.

Authorities said the car appeared to be abandoned but reinforcements were called when a person was sighted in the vicinity.

The officials grouped at the bottom of a hill leading to the Meyer homestead. Neighbors described Meyer as an elderly man "who hardly ever left home."

— Journal, Jan. 28, 1958

Following the developments quickly, the Journal reported in its next edition less than an hour later (3:24 p.m.):

Man Shot to Death In Bennet Farmhouse

And the story that followed reported:

A man was found shot to death in the August Meyer farm home two miles east of Bennet by 20 law enforcement officials that surrounded the home Tuesday afternoon.

Several tear gas bombs were fired into the home by authorities before they entered the house.

The authorities surrounded the home after a report that two Lincoln teenagers wanted for questioning in connection with an apparent triple murder may have been at the house.

No other persons were found in the home and the dead man was not immediately identified. Meyer was an elderly bachelor who neighbors said, "hardly ever left home."

The Nebraska Safety Patrol said it was possible that the Lincoln teenagers may be driving a 1950 black Ford which was driven by Robert Jensen, 17, a Bennet youth also reported missing Monday night.

Officials from the Lancaster County Sheriff's Office, the Nebraska Safety Patrol and the Lincoln City Police closed in on the home while about 30 local residents watched from a distance.

— *Journal, Jan. 28, 1958*

That story was quickly updated to identify the victim:

A man identified by officers as August Meyer has been found shot to death on his farm near Bennet.

The man's body was found as law enforcement officers moved into the house, in search of two teenagers being sought for questioning in connection with an apparent triple murder.

Reports from the scene indicated that the man's body had been dragged from the house to a small washroom. There was blood in the snow, it was reported. Before converging the officers had fired nine tear gas bombs, making it impossible to search the entire house immediately

However, two shotguns were found on a couch in the northwest corner of the house.

It was not yet known if anyone else was in the house.

After the officers had converged on the house, Louis Meyer, brother of the dead man, asked, "Did they find him?"

"Yes," was the reply.

"Oh, my God," Meyer said.

The authorities surrounded the home after a report that two Lincoln teenagers wanted for questioning in connection with an apparent triple murder may have been at the house.

— *Journal, Jan. 28, 1958*

And at the next opportunity (4:04 p.m. press time), the Journal's top headline had been changed to:

Bennet Farmer Found Slain; Youths Sought

Then (press time 5:06 p.m., more than an hour later than usual), in the final edition of the Journal for that gruesome day, came the real shocker — of which a suspicion had been given in earlier reports about the missing Bennet teen-agers:

Lincoln Murder Count Runs Up to 6 Persons

The beginning of the story now reported:

Two more bodies have been found near a farm east of Bennet, according to reports from the scene.

State Safety Patrol confirmed that they were the bodies of two Bennet teenagers missing since Monday evening.

The bodies were found by Everett Broening, a farmer in the area. The girl, observers said, was partly nude. Rifle shells were found along the road near the place the bodies had been dumped into a cellar.

This brings to six the number of bodies found since three bodies were found Monday afternoon in Belmont.

And it brings the total to three dead persons in the Bennet area, where the body of farmer August Meyer was found earlier Tuesday afternoon.

The missing Bennet couple were identified as Carol King, 16, and Robert Jensen, 17.

Both of the Bennet youngsters were juniors at Bennet High School.

The Safety Patrol reported late Tuesday afternoon that it was placing motor patrols in the Douglas-Burr-Sterling area in the search for the missing teenagers.

Carol was the daughter of Mrs. Mabel King. Robert was the son of Mr. and Mrs. Robert Jensen. Both youngsters were natives of Bennet.

Carol's father died about a month ago, Bennet residents said.

The bodies of the boy and girl were found in a cellar of a razed school house on the Meyer farm.

Search of the farm came about after officers located a car, be-

ABOVE: August Meyer, a friend of the Starkweather family, was found slain in his farmhouse near Bennet. **LEFT:** The bodies of two Bennet teen-agers, Carol King and Robert Jensen, were discovered in this abandoned storm cellar near the site of a rural Bennet schoolhouse that had been torn down earlier.

lieved to have been driven by two other teenagers wanted for questioning in connection in an apparent triple murder at 924 Belmont in Lincoln.

— Journal, Jan. 28, 1958

In The Star's newsroom, city editor Dyer had come in early because of the developing story. Shortly after 4 p.m. he learned of the three additional bodies. More staff members were assigned; photographers (who worked for both Journal and Star newsrooms) had been on duty all day as developments occurred.

The Star's story the next morning was headlined again in the biggest type available to the paper (inch-and-a-half letters, with a second line of one-inch letters).

3 MORE BODIES FOUND
Bennet Victims Bring Toll To 6

At the top of the story was a brief insert in bold type that announced:

Patrol Checks Leads

State Safety Patrolmen worked relentlessly throughout the night Tuesday following leads they hoped would end in the apprehension of Charles Starkweather, wanted for questioning in the murder of six persons in the Lincoln area.

One of the tips that sounded promising prompted a chase after a car that roughly matched the description of the one Starkweather is thought to be driving. Even the last two numbers in the license plate matched the ones on the car sought. The car was finally stopped near Humboldt. No connection was found between the car or its occupants and the missing Lincoln youths.

— Star, Jan. 29, 1958

The main story reported:

Lawmen in seven states pressed a search Tuesday night for two Lincoln teenagers who are wanted in connection with what authorities call the most shocking series of murders in Nebraska history.

Six persons were dead — five shot to death and a 2-year-old girl fatally clubbed.

Being sought in connection with the crimes are Caril Ann Fugate, 15, of 924 Belmont, and her boyfriend, Charles Starkweather,

19, whose last known address was 425 No. 10th. Police broadcasts refer to them as "armed and dangerous."

Lancaster County Attorney Scheele said Tuesday night that he will definitely file first degree charges against both Caril Fugate and Starkweather Wednesday morning.

Dead are Caril's mother and stepfather, Mr. and Mrs. Marion S. Bartlett and their 2-year-old daughter, all of 924 Belmont; August Meyer, 70, bachelor farmer near Bennet; and Robert Jensen, 17, and his 16-year-old girlfriend, Carol King, both of Bennet.

County Attorney Scheele reported late Tuesday night that a preliminary autopsy showed that Miss King "was the victim of an unnatural sex attack." He added that she and Jensen apparently died as the result of small caliber bullet wounds in the head.

Authorities believe Starkweather and Caril Fugate had fled in the 1950 dark blue Ford owned by Jensen. The four-door car is reported to have twin aerials on the rear and bears 1957 Nebraska license 2-8743.

More than 20 Safety Patrol cars from Lincoln, Omaha, Hastings, Grand Island and Fremont were making an extensive search of the Lincoln-Bennet area for the missing Lincoln couple.

Latest victims of the apparent murder spree — for which authorities have found no definite motive — were Jensen and Carol King. Their bodies were discovered about 4 p.m. Tuesday in the storm cellar of a rural school which was razed about two months ago.

The cellar is located about one mile from the farm of August Meyer — and his farm is just two miles east of Bennet.

Jensen and Miss King had gone out on a date about 7:30 p.m. Monday, saying they would be gone only a short time. When they did not return home police were notified. Bennet area residents reported the young couple often parked on the road which goes past the razed school.

Scheele said Jensen was shot several times, Miss King once. The autopsy further showed, as expected, that Meyer died from a shotgun wound to the head. Scheele also said the autopsy on the Bartletts showed they had been dead at least since Saturday night.

Everett Broening, who farms near the former school site where the youths' bodies were found, decided to check the storm cellar after he became curious about a car he heard accelerate at high speed away from the school site area about 10 p.m. Monday. At first he had thought nothing of it, but when Meyer's body was found he decided to investigate.

Broening took off the cellar cover and discovered the bodies of the two youths — the body of the girl was nearly nude but Jensen was fully clothed.

Authorities had gone to the Meyer farm about 2 p.m. when the

Starkweather's car was spotted parked in a lane leading to the farm home.

After firing nine tear gas bombs into Meyer's house lawmen entered and the house ransacked but empty. Meyer's body was then found in an adjacent washhouse.

Meyer apparently had been shot with a shotgun blast and Jensen and Miss King with a rifle. A .410 shotgun shell was found near Meyer's body and several .22 caliber shells were found near the cellar.

The bodies of Bartlett, 57, his wife Velda, 37, and their daughter were found Monday about 4:30 p.m. in two outbuildings at the rear of their home at 924 Belmont. A search was then begun for Caril Fugate and Starkweather. A relative had been denied entrance to the Bartlett home by Caril Monday morning.

— Star, Jan. 29, 1958

That main story was written by Star police reporter Del Harding, who had written the previous day's page one story and who was to continue handling the lead stories through both of the murder trials that followed. That night he also wrote a story carried on an inside page outlining the timetable of events up to that point.

Meanwhile, Star reporter Nancy Benjamin had dashed to the nearby little town of Bennet, where the latest bodies had been found. Printed alongside pictures of the victims, the fugitives, the farmhouse and the old schoolhouse storm cellar where the new victims were found, her story examined the effects of the continually expanding murder case on the tiny village:

BENNET, Neb. — This village was an armed fortress Tuesday night fearing another onslaught by the Lincoln couple believed to have been involved in the slaying of three Bennet residents.

Hardware store operator Herbert Randall reported that the 400 town residents and surrounding farm families "all have guns and won't mind using them."

Tuesday night a group of about 30 men armed with shotguns and rifles stopped in the store for ammunition. They planned a search "foot-by-foot" of the surrounding coutryside for the slayers of two Bennet high school students who had been "out on a date" when last seen.

Third of the "senseless slayings" was a 70-year-old bachelor farmer, August Meyer, "a man who minded his own business," according to R.E. Clark, Bennet editor.

Most of the Bennet community remained indoors with guns handy, although there had been no recent report of the hunted pair being sighted in the area.

Activity outdoors during the night-long search for the pair was mainly on the part of Lincoln, county and state law officers combing the territory and checking abandoned buildings and lonely farmhouses.

The teenage son of Everett Broening, dairy farmer who found

the Bennet teenagers' bodies, told The Star that the Bennet High School boy and girl found shot in an old school storm cave Tuesday afternoon, had been "going steady" before their sudden deaths.

The boy described the Bennet couple as "about the most popular kids in school" and told of 16-year-old Carol King's good grades and fine singing in the school choir. Mr. Broening described the dead girl as "a pretty, slender little girl."

The slain youth, Bob Jensen, was also described by the Bennet youth as "real popular" with the 56 other high school students. Both the teenagers were juniors in high school.

The elder Broening, describing his finding of the bodies said, "I don't think they were beaten . . . but they must have been dragged into the cave because there was blood and trampled ground around the entrance."

One Bennet resident told The Star that "he knew for sure" that Jensen's car, believed taken by the Lincoln teenagers, had a nearly full gas tank. He said he had seen the youth fill the tank Monday.

Residents pointed out that several identifying marks and special accessories would aid in spotting Jensen's car. A minor accident recently caused repair work on the front bumper and that part of the front grille of the 1950 dark blue Ford was missing.

The car has twin antennae on the rear fenders and white side-wall tires, according to a local garageman. Black primer paint is visible on the car trunk edges.

Telephone lines were jammed in the small Bennet community, and operators reported that residents were phoning relatives in other states to tell them of their safety, as well as checking the most recent news of the small town tragedy.

Carl Saunders, a Lincoln business man who lives in Bennet, said he was playing cards with Robert Jensen Sr., Monday night when Carol King's mother called to ask if Jensen had seen the young couple.

Saunders said he and Jensen went out looking for the couple and even visited the area near the schoolhouse site where the bodies were found. Young folks in the area often go out to that vicinity and park, Saunders said.

The parents of young Jensen operate a general store in Bennet. The family has lived in the Bennet area several generations.

Tuesday marked the second time this month that death has struck in the King family. The girl's father, Russell King, died unexpectedly Jan. 3 in Lincoln. Her mother, Mrs. Mabel King, recently moved from the King farm near Bennet into town.

Both Carol and Robert were described as "very popular with other students" in Bennet high. Young Jensen was forced to cut his participation in athletics this past year due to effects of polio. The youth was hospitalized for many months several years ago when struck by the disease. Robert was a member of the Bennet football team during his sophomore year.

Carol was also prominent in extra curricular activities in school. In addition to her mother she is survived by a brother, Warren of Bennet; a sister, Mrs. LaVerne L. Stolte of Lincoln; and her grandfather, M.L. King of Bennet.

Robert's survivors include his parents; a brother, Dewey of Bennet; two grandmothers, Mrs. Lucille Bratt and Mrs. Bessie Jensen, both of Bennet; and two great grandmothers, Mrs. Cora Beavers and Mrs. Gertrude Kuse, also of Bennet.

Meyer's survivors include a brother, Louis of Bennet, and three sisters, Mrs. Clara Jones of Bennet, Mrs. Mary Davis of Nebraska City and Mrs. Charles Stortz of Lincoln.

— Star, Jan. 29, 1958

Before she had been sent to cover the situation in Bennet, Nancy Benjamin also had interviewed Starkweather's landlady and written that story for an inside page. She was to continue handling interviews and feature stories on the case for the next half-dozen years.

The death toll now stood at six. But there was more to come.

MORE BODIES, MORE HEADLINES

For Neale Copple's staff in the Lincoln Journal newsroom, Wednesday began with a calm that was only relative and that would be shattered before the day was over.

Staff members were still grappling with one of their biggest stories ever, and the Journal's first edition headline (press start 9:01 a.m.) reported:

Brutal Killer of 6 Still at Large

Three Slain Near Bennet, Murders Shock Entire Country

The text of that story, as well as the headline, abandoned the cautious terminology used in earlier stories, as the county attorney announced he definitely would file charges:

> While the nation watched, police from Nebraska and nearby states conducted a manhunt they hoped would end "the most shocking series of murders in Nebraska's history."
>
> Hundreds of reports came in as people in several states thought they had seen the teenage couple sought for questioning in connection with the six deaths.
>
> Being sought in connection with the series of crimes are Caril Ann Fugate, 15, of 924 Belmont and her boyfriend, Charles Starkweather, 19, whose last known address was 425 N. 10th.
>
> Law officials broadcasts refer to the couple as "armed and dangerous."
>
> Known dead are:
>
> Mrs. Velda Bartlett, 36, of 924 Belmont.
>
> Mr. Marion Bartlett, 58, of 924 Belmont.
>
> Betty Jean Bartlett, 2, of 924 Belmont.
>
> August Meyer, 70, Bennet.
>
> Carol King, 16, of Bennet.
>
> Robert Jensen, 17, of Bennet.
>
> At last reports authorities still believed Starkweather and Caril Fugate were in the 1950 dark blue Ford owned by Jensen. The four-door car is reported to have twin aerials on the rear fender and bears the license 2-8743.
>
> County Attorney Scheele said Tuesday night that he will definitely file first degree murder charges against both the girl and Starkweather Wednesday morning.
>
> The Lancaster County attorney reported late Tuesday night that a preliminary autopsy showed that Miss King "was the victim of an unnatural sex attack."
>
> He added that she and Jensen apparently died as the result of

small caliber bullet wounds in the head.

Jensen and King were the latest victims of the apparent murder spree — for which authorities have found no definite motive.

Their bodies were discovered about 4 p.m. Tuesday in a storm cellar of a rural school that was razed about two months ago.

Bennet residents said Jensen and Miss King had gone out on a date about 7:30 p.m. Monday, saying they would be gone only a short time.

Denny Nelson, service station attendant, said Jensen came into the station about 7 p.m. Monday and got $3 worth of gasoline.

Everett Broening, who farms near the razed rural school, was the first to find Jensen and King.

He said, "I just happened to check that old storm cellar on a hunch."

The cellar is located about one mile from the farm of August Meyer, whose farm is just about two miles east of Bennet.

Broening took off the cellar cover and discovered the bodies of the two youths.

The body of the girl was nearly nude but Jensen was fully clothed.

— Journal, Jan. 29, 1958

With that first edition story out of the way, the Journal had this staff lineup at noon:

■ Two reporters at police headquarters, one in the sheriff's office and one at Safety Patrol headquarters — all with orders to call in every 15 minutes whether they had anything fresh to report or not.

■ Two reporters in the newsroom monitoring the three police radio bands.

■ Six reporters on rewrite checking out the most likely police reports on the search for the car Starkweather was believed driving.

■ One rewriteman assigned to put together the main, running story.

■ Three reporters in cars checking in person the most likely police leads.

In an article for the state press association magazine, Copple later described the situation:

"At 12:30 p.m. a police reporter called in that Assistant Police Chief Gene Masters had gone 'somewhere in a helluva hurry.'

"A few minutes later a rewriteman called the Ward home as one of several addresses being broadcast by police. Masters answered, told the reporter to 'get the hell off the phone,' and hung up.

"At 12:49 p.m. a Journal staffer at the Wards' reported that the missing car was there. That was 26 minutes before the 1:15 p.m. second edition (7,000 press run) foundry time for page one. . . .

"At 12:50 p.m. the reporter at the scene reported three more bodies found.

"At 12:55 p.m. he identified them as the Wards and their maid."

That next edition of the Journal (for which the press actually started at 1:30 p.m.) carried the headline:

3 More Lincolnites Found Dead

And the story that followed, pieced together quickly with no time for proof-reading, reported:

> Three more Lincolnites were found dead Wednesday afternoon at the Lauer Ward home at 2843 S. 28th in Lincoln, according to Sheriff Merle Karnopp. This brings to nine the number of persons slain in Lancaster County in "the most shocking series of murders in Nebraska's history."
>
> Latest victims were identified as:
>
> C. Lauer Ward, about 50, president of Capital Bridge Co.
>
> Clara, his wife.
>
> The Wards' maid, tentatively identified only as "Lillian."
>
> Sheriff Karnopp said apparent cause of death was gun shot.
>
> The blue Ford which Starkweather was thought to be driving was found in the garage.
>
> Discovery of the apparent murders came after a blue 1950 Ford earlier driven by 17-year-old Robert Jensen of Bennet, one of the nine slain, was found at the Ward home.
>
> Police said a 1956 black Packard sedan, 1957 Nebraska license number 2-17415, was also reported stolen from the Ward home. It was registered to the Capital Steel Co.
>
> Officers said "it is believed" to be driven by Starkweather and Miss Fugate.
>
> While the search for 14-year-old Caril Ann Fugate and her boy-friend, 19-year-old Charles Starkweather, continued, Nebraskans were shocked as they followed the trail of violence that first appeared Monday night in Lincoln.
>
> The two, both charged with first degree murder, are wanted for questioning in connection with the killing of a total of six known Lancaster County residents.
>
> — *Journal, Jan. 29, 1958*

Copple's magazine report on the scene continued:

"Rewrite produced biographies and cuts from the library.

"Associate editor Joe R. Seacrest, reading page proof on the editorial page, corrected the number dead and their names in the lead editorial.

"At 1:02 p.m. the search was on for the Packard Starkweather was now believed driving — possibly still in Lincoln — and a metropolitan city panicked."

A bulletin inserted into a split run of that edition at 1:54 p.m. reported:

Mayor to Call Out N. Guard
Mayor Abe Martin said he and the sheriff were going to have the governor call out the national guard in the search for the murderer.

And another story reported that Caril Fugate "may have been killed" and that two men were specifically assigned to search for the girl.

That story also reported between 40 and 50 sheriff's deputies, farmers and State Safety Patrolmen were searching the county for the pair. Sheriff Merle Karnopp said, "If we don't shake them today they're probably out of the county." He did not know they already were far away.

In the next edition (on the press at 2:50 p.m.) the Journal boosted its page-wide headline to two lines:

3 More Bodies Found to Boost Murders to 9; Guard Called Out

Sidebars on the front page reported other developments:

Troops To Help In Hunt
Gov. Victor E. Anderson has mobilized the Nebraska National Guard Wednesday afternoon to help hunt down the teenage youths sought in the murder of nine people.

The governor's action came on the heels of the discovery of three more victims in Lincoln.

Anderson said he called Col. Hob Turner and that as many guardsmen as are needed would be mobilized.

The guard will work under Col. C.J. Sanders, head of the Nebraska Safety Patrol.

Anderson said the guardsmen would be coordinated with Lincoln police, Lancaster County Sheriff's officers and the patrol.

The governor's office said that between 100 and 200 men would be called out.

Gov. Victor Anderson said the mobilization of the Guard is under way and will be completed as soon as the forces can be called.

Col. Turner conferred with law enforcement officials to see how the Guard can fit into the capture plans.

— *Journal, Jan. 29, 1958*

Panic and Terror Grip Lincoln
Lincoln was a city of panic Wednesday in the midst of the fren-

The National Guard was called out to patrol Lincoln streets.

Neighbors, reporters and lawmen gather at the Ward home.

zied pursuit of a gun-crazed killer who has left nine murder victims in the city and surrounding area.

— Lincoln stores reported they were doing a rushing business in the sale of firearms.

— Armed men, obviously prepared to protect their homes, were reported standing in yards in widely-scattered parts of the city.

Police were blocking all roads leading out of the city as hundreds of calls were received reporting the sighting of black Packards, fitting the description of that missing from the Ward residence.

Police put most stock in a report of a black Packard heading south on 14th Street.

Following the discovery of three more victims — Lincoln industrialist C. Lauer Ward, his wife and maid — the city was virtually blockaded by police.

Gov. Victor Anderson called out the National Guard and between 100 and 200 men were mobilizing in the search for Charles Starkweather, 19, and Caril Fugate, 14. The couple earlier were being sought in connection with seven other murders in the Lincoln area.

— Hundreds of reports were received from over the city of the sighting of a black Packard similar to that missing from the Ward residence.

The State Safety Patrol had highways south and southeast of Lincoln covered with patrol cars.

— The suspected get-away car was reported sighted between Mullen and Whitman in the Nebraska Sandhills at 5:10 a.m., and at Alliance at 8 a.m.

One of the most reliable reports of the Ward car came from a truck driver, Maynard Behrens of Broken Bow. He told the Safety Patrol he saw what was believed to be the car at Mullen, Whitman and Alliance.

He said he turned a spotlight on the truck and the license number read: 2-17415, the number of the Ward car.

— Journal, Jan. 29, 1958

Then, only an hour before the deadline for the big city edition, the Journal added two pages to its paper and filled them with pictures and stories. That edition's pages were completed at 3:10 p.m., 35 minutes later than usual. The presses never started.

At 3:25 came the bulletin that Starkweather had been caught in Wyoming.

Headlines in the new city edition (the press started at 3:35 p.m.) screamed:

Killer Wounded in Wyoming; 3 More Bodies; 9 Now Murdered

And a separate wire story from Douglas, Wyo., carried the first details of the capture. With new information added in the final edition at 4:50 p.m. that day, the story read:

Girl Also Captured Unhurt

DOUGLAS, Wyo. (AP) — A man was wounded and captured near Douglas Wednesday and a Wyoming deputy sheriff identified him as Charles Starkweather, 19, wanted in connection with nine slayings in Nebraska.

Deputy Sheriff Bill Romer, who identified him, said the man suffered "a superficial head wound." He was placed in the Converse County jail here.

Romer said a girl was with Starkweather. He did not identify her. She apparently was not hurt.

Another official said she was Caril Fugate, Starkweather's 14-year-old girlfriend.

Officers said the body of a man was found near this eastern Wyoming town. He was not immediately identified nor was the cause of death learned at once.

Romer, en route to Douglas on another matter, related that he had met Starkweather's car at Ayers natural bridge about 5 miles west of Douglas and that a "running gun battle" ensued. Starkweather was wounded slightly, he said.

Douglas is about 500 miles from the Lincoln area — at the time of capture the scene of the largest manhunt in the state's history.

Starkweather was captured at 3 p.m. CST, only three hours after the latest three bodies of the string of nine victims had been found.

The capture was listed as "just west of Douglas."

Ken Sackett, an official of the State Department of Revenue in Casper, told the Safety Patrol in Lincoln that the Fugate girl was also in custody. He said she broke away from Starkweather during the capture and reached deputies.

The girl said she had been held by Starkweather since they left Lincoln and she feared he was "going to take me to Washington state and kill me."

Sackett also said Starkweather had shot and killed another person in Wyoming — a civilian, not an officer. Sackett said the shooting did not take place during the capture.

The capture came not long after Nebraska authorities insisted Starkweather was still in Lincoln.

Up until the reported shooting in Wyoming, the latest victims had been a Lincoln businessman, his wife and their maid.

— Journal, Jan. 29, 1958

The afternoon the Wards' bodies were found, Journal city editor Neale Copple remembers, a reporter turned up at his desk. Copple reminded him he was supposed to be with the police and asked what he was doing in the office. The answer: "Just look at me." The reporter was short, freckled, red-haired — the same as Charles Starkweather. "And," he said, "I drive a dark Packard, and it's double-parked outside, and I'm not going out there."

The harried Copple found something else for his Starkweather-double to do.

In The Star's newsroom that afternoon the news staff also attempted to follow developments, but Star deadlines for the next morning's editions were later, so there was not the same deadline pressure. There did have to be decisions about how to deploy a limited (and becoming weary) staff.

Star city editor Earl Dyer remembers that Nancy Benjamin, always a feisty and ambitious reporter, wanted to go to the Ward neighborhood and ring doorbells to get neighbors' reactions and any facts they might know. But with his mind on the number of weapons being sold in gun stores and being displayed on the streets, Dyer ordered her to stay in the office — telephone interviews with the neighbors might be less impressive in the next morning's paper but it would be safer.

That afternoon Star publisher Walter W. White paid a visit to the newsroom.

Dyer, ever conscious of the paper's policy of trying to avoid overtime work at higher pay, told White, "I've no idea how much overtime we're running up," to which White replied, "The last thing you are to worry about right now is the overtime."

In an unusual extravagance, the two newspapers chartered a plane to carry a photographer and reporters to Wyoming.

The next morning's Star carried the headline:

CAPTURE IN WYOMING ENDS THREE-DAY REIGN OF TERROR

Starkweather And Caril Fugate Caught After 10th Killing

The main story, pieced together from Lincoln and Wyoming sources and wire service reports, told the story:

> The Lincoln area's three-day reign of terror that saw nine persons wantonly slain in an almost unbelievable chain of events ended at 3:30 Wednesday afternoon when 19-year-old Charles Starkweather was captured by two Wyoming lawmen.
>
> His empty .38 caliber revolver at his side, he told officers, "If I had had a gun, I'd have shot you."
>
> He suffered head cuts during an exchange of shots with a deputy sheriff. With Starkweather was Caril Fugate, the 14-year-old girl who fled with him from the Lincoln area where police say he killed nine people. Included among the victims were Caril's parents.
>
> A tenth murder victim was found not far from where Starkweather was captured. Sheriff's men said he admitted the killing. The dead man was Merle Collison, 37-year-old Great Falls, Mont., shoe salesman, the Associated Press reported.
>
> There were rumors around the jail that Starkweather signed a statement admitting the slaying of Collison and wrote out an admission of the Nebraska killings. The rumors were not confirmed by any officials.
>
> Starkweather's nine Lincoln area victims discovered over a three-day period included: C. Lauer Ward, 47, of 2843 S. 24th, his wife, Clara O., and housekeeper, Lillian Fencl, 51, found about noon Wednesday.
>
> August Meyer, 70, living near Bennet; Carol King, 16, of Bennet and Robert Jensen, 17, of Bennet, found Tuesday afternoon.
>
> Marion S. Bartlett, 58, of 924 Belmont, his wife, Velda, 36, and

their daughter, Betty Jean, 2½, found Monday afternoon.

The two teenagers were run to earth in rugged country where Old West gunmen often holed up.

The girl was almost hysterical and ran fleeing to Deputy Sheriff Bill Romer crying out her fear Starkweather would kill her. She was in a state of shock shortly afterward.

Romer said she screamed to him:

"He's going to kill me. He's crazy. He just killed a man!"

Romer said the gunman, who likes to swagger in cowboy boots and black motorcycle jacket, had made a crude attempt to disguise his flaming red hair with shoe polish.

Lancaster County Atty. Elmer Scheele said in Lincoln that he and two officers will fly to Wyoming Thursday to seek extradition of Starkweather to Nebraska.

"We're going to do our utmost to get him back here," Scheele said.

Wyoming, if it chooses, will have priority on prosecuting Starkweather in the slaying of Collison.

Despite Starkweather's capture, Lincoln Mayor Bennett Martin said, "We're still in a damn sick situation. We still don't know whether the number of victims will stop at nine."

The bloody trail began less than 48 hours ago in Lincoln when the slaying of Caril's parents and infant half-sister was discovered. As police pressed investigation, other killings were disclosed until the total reached nine. The hunt was started for Starkweather but he and the girl escaped the frantic search.

As National Guardsmen culled the byways of Lincoln, the stolen car driven by Starkweather was speeding west across the state line and into Wyoming. Behind them police ran down false leads in a desperate effort to nab Starkweather before any further violence occurred.

Douglas Sheriff Earl Heflin derided the tough talk of Starkweather, who snarled after his capture:

"They wouldn't have caught me if I hadn't stopped. If I'd had a gun, I'd have shot them."

Heflin said that when Starkweather stopped his car and was caught, "He thought he was bleeding to death. That's the kind of yellow S.O.B. he is." Flying glass from car windows smashed by bullets in the short flight cut his scalp.

Heflin said a first degree murder charge would be filed Thursday morning against Starkweather in the killing of Collison.

No decision as to whether to try Starkweather in Wyoming or release him to Nebraska authorities has been reached, he said.

Starkweather faces multiple murder charges which could mean the death penalty in either state. Wyoming executes condemned slayers in the gas chamber and in Nebraska death in the electric chair is the supreme penalty. In the latter state, the jury sets the death penalty.

In Wyoming, however, Governor Wilward Simpson opposes the death penalty and has said publicly he will continue to spare condemned murderers.

Converse County Attorney William Dixon said that Collison had apparently been napping in his car when Starkweather drove up.

"Starkweather shot once through the window of the car and said 'come out,'" Dixon related. "Then he blasted him (Collison) five or six times." Dixon said Starkweather told him he wanted Collison's car because his own was "too hot."

An oil company worker Joe Sprinkle of Casper, drove up to the scene while Starkweather was still there and stopped to investigate. The fugitive shoved a .22 rifle in Sprinkle's face and the two began to wrestle.

Casper Deputy Sheriff Romer was on a rent receipt inspection job when he spotted two men fighting over a gun near two stalled cars. One was Sprinkle, fighting for his life. As Romer pulled up, Starkweather ran for his car. The Fugate girl fled from the getaway car and ran screaming to Romer.

Romer radioed for a roadblock which was flung up hastily but Starkweather roared through it at more than 100 miles an hour. Sheriff Heflin and an officer gave chase, firing at the car. It careened through Douglas and five miles out of town pulled to a stop.

The sullen gunman offered no resistance. He had a .32 caliber pistol with him. It was empty.

Back at the scene of the struggle, Sprinkle stood near the parked car. Shoved down under the dashboard was the body of Collison.

The Casper oil employee was short and to the point about why he had jumped Starkweather. He had stopped because the two cars were parked and he thought somebody needed help.

When Starkweather jammed the rifle in his face Sprinkle grabbed it.

"All I saw was the gun barrel and every time I looked it got bigger," he said. Sprinkle is a husky 185-pounder and he won the deadly tug-of-war with the 5-foot-5 gunman. Then, Sprinkle said he found the rifle had already been emptied.

In a Douglas jail cell Starkweather slouched on his bunk glowering. A Casper newsman who was nearby said Starkweather asserted he had shot his Nebraska victims in self defense.

"What would you do if they tried to come at you?" newsman Phil Mcauley quoted Starkweather.

As night closed in over this cattle town, a strict guard was set over Starkweather. The Fugate girl, who Starkweather said had been forced by him to go along, was under sedation.

— Star, Jan. 30, 1958

The Star's front page illustrated the story with large photos of both Starkweather and Fugate after their capture, and accompanied the main story with a bylined sidebar from police reporter Del Harding, now in Wyoming:

Caril Fugate Says: 'Family Dead Nearly Week'

DOUGLAS, Wyo. — The Bartlett family lay dead for almost a week as a group of teenage boys, led by Charles Starkweather, plotted to rob a Lincoln bank.

That's what the semi-hysterical Caril Fugate told Deputy Sheriff Bill Romer of Natrona County, Wyo., just after she and Starkweather were captured here. She said her family was killed a week ago Tuesday.

She said she was an unwilling hostage at all times during the plotting and subsequent murders.

She added that the other three boys, after spending an unspecified time at the Bartlett home, "chickened out" and left only Starkweather with her in the home.

She also implicated Starkweather in the Dec. 1 slaying of service station attendant Robert Colvert. She said she was involved but had not actually done the shooting.

She said she witnessed every one of the nine murders in Lincoln and Bennet.

Every time someone came to 924 Belmont, Starkweather stood behind the door with a gun and made her get rid of them.

This included a Saturday morning visit from police, who had been summoned by relatives who were disturbed at not hearing from the Bartletts.

When Mrs. Bartlett's mother, Mrs. Pansy Street, tried to get in Monday morning and was refused she left with a threat to get a search warrant. This was when Starkweather and she left, beginning a flight that culminated in seven more murders.

She said the pair fled Lincoln Tuesday night after the slayings of Mr. and Mrs. C. Lauer Ward and their housekeeper.

Other details of the gruesome chain of death were not made clear by the girl before she lapsed into shock and was put under sedation, Deputy Romer said.

Lincoln police officials late Wednesday, however, said there were indications that the Bartletts were alive after the Tuesday mentioned by Caril. They did not elaborate.

— Star, Jan. 30, 1958

That front page marked the end of the violence, but only the beginning of a story that was to continue to capture the attention of local newspaper readers for years to come.

TIME FOR DETAILS

Thursday of "murder week" found the newspapers struggling to piece together the story of what had happened. Star and Journal staff members, tired to the bone, knuckled down to the task of unearthing every possible detail. Lincoln wanted those details, and it got them from the two papers — columns and columns of details. The community also was beginning to ask whether law enforcement officers had done all they could as early as they could.

Douglas, a Wyoming community of about 3,000 people, was the news capital of the nation as its sheriff, its police chief and other witnesses told their stories of the capture to reporters. One story said there were about 30 reporters in Douglas, from all across the nation.

The Journal's first edition Thursday morning carried this account of the capture, pieced together from interviews with Converse County Sheriff Earl Heflin, Douglas Police Chief Robert C. Ainslie and Natrona County Deputy Sheriff William Romer of Casper:

> The Lincoln youth apparently drove through Douglas headed west on Highway 87, at about 2 p.m. Wednesday.
>
> Twelve miles west of Douglas at the intersection of Highways 87, 20 and 26 and near a turnoff to Ayres Natural Bridge they came upon a shoe salesman identified as Merle Collison, who was sleeping in his 1956 Buick, parked alongside the highway, according to Deputy Converse County Sheriff John William Owens.
>
> Collison, who had identification papers listing Great Falls, Mont., as his address but was driving an automobile with Oregon license plates, was apparently pulled from his car and shot, Owens said.
>
> An autopsy later revealed he was shot once in the nose, once in the cheek, once in the neck, twice in the cheek, once in the left arm, once in the right wrist and twice in the left leg with a .22 caliber rifle, Dixon said.
>
> Immediately after the shooting Joe Sprinkle of Casper, a geologist, came upon the scene, stopped, and when he saw what had occurred he wrestled for the rifle from Starkweather.
>
> Just as this happened, Natrona County Deputy Sheriff William Romer of Casper, on his way back to Douglas on another matter, stopped at the scene. Starkweather, Romer said, jumped back into the 1956 black Packard missing from Lincoln, and headed back toward Douglas. Miss Fugate, however, ran to Romer's car and told him that Starkweather "had held me hostage."
>
> Romer said Miss Fugate ran to him and said, "Save me. He's going to shoot me, too."
>
> "I was afraid he was going to take me to Washington and kill me," she said.
>
> Romer radioed to Douglas and Sheriff Heflin, Ainslie, Owens Wyoming Safety Patrolman Dan Webster and Game Warden Jim

Coyner answered the call.

Ainslie and Heflin, in the police chief's car, headed west on Highway 87 and came upon Starkweather about five miles west of the city. They turned around and followed the Packard at high rates of speed which Ainslie described as "120 miles an hour or faster."

When the chase reached the city limits, Starkweather was forced to slow down for traffic which was stopped for a red light, Chief Ainslie said.

"He cut to the right of the traffic and recut around to the left," the police chief said. "We hooked bumpers on the opposite side of the traffic but he got away anyway."

"Then we chased him down Fourth St. and the sheriff who had a .30-30 rifle and a .45 caliber revolver shot several times at the auto's tires. This did not stop him so the sheriff fired through the back window of the car," he added.

The chase continued through Douglas and then east on the highway, authorities said.

About three miles out of town and after Sheriff Heflin said he

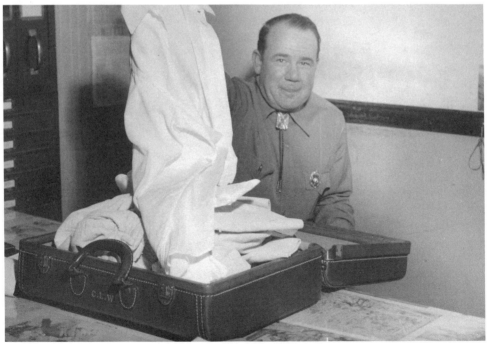

Natrona County (Wyoming) Deputy Sheriff William Romer came upon Starkweather and Fugate on the road near Douglas, Wyo.

had shot "at least a dozen times" at the auto, Starkweather came to a sudden stop in the middle of the highway.

"We stopped about 100 yards back of him and when he got out we hollered at him to to raise his hands. He didn't do it so we shot at his feet. He started to reach for his shirt so we shot again at his feet," the sheriff said.

"He still didn't raise his hands so I shot again and then he laid face down on the ground." Ainslie said: "We went up to him, shackled him and brought him back to jail. He didn't offer a bit of resistance after that."

"I'll never know why he just stopped in the road like that," Sheriff Heflin said. "He didn't even pull off the side of the road."

The sheriff said one of his shots apparently caused a piece of flying glass from the Packard's rear window to strike Starkweather on his ear cutting him slightly. He had no other injuries.

, Sheriff Heflin quoted Starkweather as saying, "They wouldn't have caught me if I hadn't stopped. If I had a gun, I would have shot them." The youth appeared "very friendly" Thursday, Heflin said.

In describing the gun battle with the youth, the sheriff said if his bullet would have been any closer, "I would have blown his head off."

Heflin said the first apparent tip which led to the capture was a report from Roy Fraham, an Ellsworth service station operator, who "on a hunch" notified authorities that the couple were in the area.

Graham said the youth was "jumpy" when he stopped at the station but "the girl was sleeping on the front seat."

Starkweather had no weapons on him when apprehended, but a .32 caliber revolver and a hunting knife were found on the seat of the Packard, Sheriff Heflin said.

The sheriff said he had no conversation with Starkweather and the youth was not interrogated.

"He is just as yellow as we figured he would be," the sheriff said. "He would tell you the time of day with your own watch."

Sheriff Heflin, who said that Starkweather had spent about an hour writing a confession, said the youth had apparently dyed his hair black with shoe polish in recent days.

The sheriff said that the statement was signed but he would not identify its content. All he would say was "it's a confession."

Heflin said Starkweather later complained that his right hand was stiff and deputies found it to be swollen.

Immediately after Starkweather was brought to jail, he told Heflin that "the girl had no part in it. Don't get rough with her."

Asked when he left Lincoln, Starkweather said, "Oh last night."

Then he was asked, "Did you drive all night?"

"Yes," he said, "and I'm tired. My ear hurts."

Miss Fugate was wearing white baton boots, slacks, a jacket and handkerchief when brought to the jail.

— Journal, Jan. 30

Geologist Joe Sprinkle's details of his part came in a separate story:

Geologist Disarms Starkweather But Finds Feat Hard to Believe

DOUGLAS, Wyo. — A 29-year-old Casper, Wyo., geologist couldn't quite believe what he had done.

Joe Sprinkle was credited by Converse County authorities with disarming 19-year-old Charles Starkweather about 12 miles west of Douglas.

"I was traveling east toward Douglas when I passed a 1956 Packard on the side of the road," he said.

"A new model Buick was facing west on the opposite side of the road. As I passed I did not see anyone in the vehicles, but I looked in my rear view mirror and saw someone get out of the Packard.

"I thought they had had an accident, so I turned my car around and came back," Sprinkle said. "I pulled in behind the Buick and I saw Starkweather open the car door. Then I asked, 'Can I help you?'

"He straightened up with a rifle he had behind him and said, 'Raise your hands. Help me release the emergency brake or I'll kill you,' " the geologist said.

"It was then I noticed the dead man behind the wheel. As I approached him, I grabbed at the gun and we fought for it in the middle of the highway. I knew that if he won I would be dead, so I managed to wrestle it (the gun) away from him," he said.

"Then he turned and ran toward the Packard and I ran for a truck which had just pulled up," Sprinkle said. "I saw the girl run from the Buick to the deputy sheriff's car."

"I had no idea who the fellow was. I only knew that he had a gun and he was going to kill me like he did this fellow in the car. I went on into Douglas to call for an ambulance. Later I met Deputy Sheriff Romer and gave him the .22 rifle I had taken."

The former Navy veteran stands five feet 11 inches, and weighs about 185.

He said he didn't want any more publicity, "I just want to be left alone," Sprinkle said.

— Journal, Jan. 30

But the bigger news by that time in Lincoln — worth a double-line headline across the top of the front page of the Journal — dealt with the first interview of Starkweather by a Nebraska officer. The headline in the 9 a.m. edition:

Solution of Colvert Murder Is Hinted After Interview With Starkweather

The story, by Journal reporter Al Remmenga, who had flown with Star reporter Del Harding and a photographer to Wyoming:

DOUGLAS, Wyo. — Lincoln Police Lt. Robert Henninger says he "has reason to believe" that the arrest of 19-year-old Charles R. Starkweather will clear up a total of 10 Lancaster County murders.

"There are indications that he was involved in the slaying of 21-year-old Robert Colvert on Dec. 1," the detective said after questioning the youth for more than two hours in his jail cell.

Meanwhile observers here said they believe that County Attorney William Dixon would not fight extradition of Starkweather to Nebraska.

He has filed murder charges against the Lincoln youth, but does not plan to file them against Caril Fugate who was with Starkweather.

And Gov. Milward Simpson said in Cheyenne that he would sign extradition papers "in a jiffy."

It was reported that Starkweather has told Douglas authorities that he would not fight extradition.

In Nebraska Gov. Victor Anderson said that he was pleased with Simpson's willingness to cooperate.

"While Starkweather did not actually admit to any shootings," Henninger said he admitted being at the Marion Bartlett home at 924 Belmont on Monday, the August Meyer home near Bennet the same day, and the C. Lauer Ward home at 2843 S. 24th on Tuesday evening.

Henninger said he "did not question him about details because I hope to get a written statement later today."

"He emphatically denies the sexual molest of 16-year-old Carol King of Bennet," the detective said.

The molestation was indicated by an autopsy after her death.

"He is still touchy and I didn't want to get too deeply into the killings because I want him to make a written statement later," Henninger said.

The officer said, "Starkweather did not describe any of the slayings except that he indicated that 2-year-old Betty Jean Bartlett was hit on the head with a gun butt."

Referring to the Colvert slaying, Henninger said, "I think we will

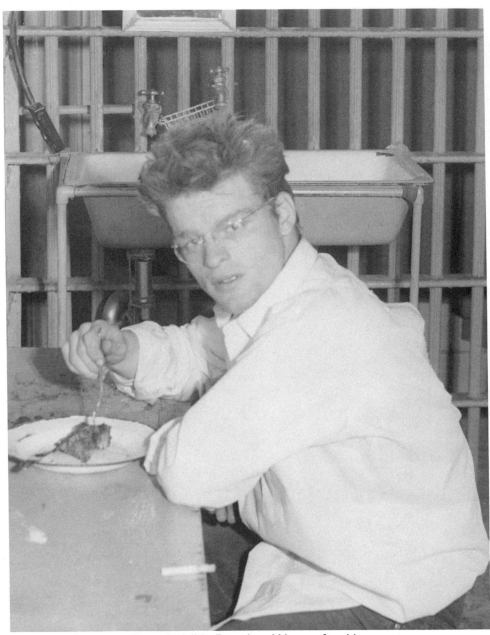

Starkweather eats dinner in jail in Douglas, Wyo., after his arrest.

be able to clean that one up."

Henninger said that Starkweather admitted being at the Ward home until about 8 p.m. Tuesday. Then, the detective said, he said he left Lincoln in Ward's 1956 Packard, drove through Seward, stopped at Grand Island for gas, and "stopped somewhere about 4:30 a.m. Wednesday and slept until about 8 in the morning."

The detective said he questioned the youth about any possible or any additional bodies in Omaha or outstate, but "Starkweather says there are none." The detective said the youth also said he had not been involved in any other crimes in the Lincoln area in recent months.

Henninger said that "Starkweather told him that the couple was headed for Washington where Starkweather said he had a brother named Leonard."

The Lincoln police officer said, "My main purpose this morning was to see if he would admit anything that we don't have yet.

"If we can get him tied down on one slaying, then we can stomp on his toes about the others."

Henninger said that Starkweather "indicated" that he would talk to Police Chief Joe Carroll, Sheriff Merle Karnopp, Co. Atty. Elmer Scheele and Safety Patrol Capt. Harold Smith who were expected to arrive in Douglas late Thursday.

Henninger, who gave the youth a pack of cigarettes, said the two-hour conference indicated to him that Starkweather may have "been mad, scared or just acting peculiar."

Starkweather did not go into the role of Caril Ann Fugate in any of the incidents about which he was questioned, Henninger said.

He noted that Lancaster County authorities still have a first degree murder charge filed against both of the teenagers.

The detective said that Starkweather was not "surly but very serious about our conversation."

— Journal, Jan. 30, 1958

Remmenga's story was the first on page one to carry a reporter's byline that week; all the previous stories had been pieced together at the Journal's news desk from different sources, so quickly had developments come.

Meanwhile, the Journal reported, the Lincoln City Council was in special session Thursday afternoon to discuss police handling of the case, and the Journal itself was not hesitant to raise questions about the matter. A front-page article by staff writer Leo Scherer in the first edition said:

Performance of Lawmen Questioned

In the wake of "the worst series of murders in midwest history" came citizens asking questions about law enforcement officials' performance in the case.

Some of the questions being asked were:

> — Why didn't police find the bodies in Belmont Saturday?
> — Were all complaints of the families involved fully investigated?
> — Could the senseless killings have been ended at just three?
> — Why were not physical roadblocks (barricades) set between Lincoln and Bennet after three bodies were discovered near Bennet Tuesday?
> — Why were Starkweather and Miss Fugate able to travel nearly the length of the state after a nation-wide alarm?
> — Why were the wanted pair always several hours ahead of law enforcement agencies?
>
> — *Journal, Jan. 30, 1958*

Relatives of both Starkweather and the victims also were quoted as questioning law enforcement activities:

> Guy Starkweather, father of Charles, commented earlier that "the police could have prevented all this. They had been warned Saturday night."
> He added Thursday to a Journal reporter that "the police had a duty to perform Saturday — they aren't carrying those pistols for nothing."
> Starkweather called police Thursday morning denying he had stated anything to the effect that Lincoln police had been ineffi-committed, according to police officers.
> Robert Von Busch, son-in-law of Mrs. Bartlett, expressed disappointment in the way the police handled the Belmont matter.
> Von Busch said he became worried when he went to the house and was told to leave because the family had the flu.
> "So I went down to the police station and told them that something was really wrong at the house," he said. "They said that the Bartletts were probably gone on vacation and they were tired of me bothering them all the time."
> He continued:
> "I knew that something was wrong so I drove back out to the house with Rodney (Charles Starkweather's brother) and checked the back of the house.
> "That's where I found the bodies. I then drove back to the police station and told the officers," Von Busch said.
> "It sure seems crazy that sick people would go on vacation leaving a 14-year-old girl behind," Von Busch added.
>
> — *Journal, Jan. 30, 1958*

In a later edition, however, that story moved to an inside page, and the headline was changed nearly 180 degrees to read: "Performance of Lawmen Supported." Now the story highlighted City Council support for the police and

Helen and Guy Starkweather, parents of Charles, with family dog.

downplayed (but still asked) the pointed questions of the Scherer article.

Another of the major questions of that week — and of the years to come — moved into headlines: Just what was Caril Fugate's role in the grisly slayings? The Journal reported the statements of the deputy county sheriff to whose car Caril ran shortly before Starkweather's capture:

Caril Fugate Tells Deputy She Was Hostage

CASPER, Wyo. — At speeds over 100 miles per hour, Caril Ann Fugate, 14, watched the last "free" moments of her boyfriend Charles Starkweather.

Natrona Deputy County Sheriff Bill Romer, one of the few people who talked to the girl before she became "too hysterical to understand" told the story:

"When I came on the scene where the young geologist and Caril were, she immediately jumped out of the Packard and ran in beside me in the front seat."

She told the deputy that Starkweather, who had left the scene at a high rate of speed a few minutes before, had "just killed a man."

Also one of the last persons who talked to the girl before she was locked in Converse County Jail, Romer said the girl looked tired and hungry and "downright afraid."

"She just sat there in a high state of excitement as I radioed ahead to try and stop him."

"I don't know how much to believe really, but I have the feeling she was telling me the truth as we tried to catch up with Starkweather."

A summary of what Romer said the girl told him:

1. "She told me she had always been a hostage but did not say one way or another that she tried to get away from Starkweather." (Starkweather had reportedly told other authorities she made "four or five attempts.")

2. She told the deputy that her home in Lincoln (Bartletts) had been the "headquarters" for a group of "two or three teenagers" with Starkweather, who planned to rob a Lincoln bank.

He said Caril Ann told him she had been captive in the Bartlett home, too, and that they (Caril and Starkweather) had left only when the other teenagers "chickened out" on the bank robbery plans.

3. "She told me that she had 'seen' all nine murders in Nebraska," Romer said.

4. "She made mention of the Colvert murder but did not indicate in any way that Starkweather was involved. She mentioned a name which both Lincoln police and we are checking out."

Romer said the girl "finally wound down" and became unintelligible.

"I couldn't tell for sure what she was saying sometimes. Her memory seemed to get progressively worse as we got her near the jail."

Romer said she complained that she had not been allowed out of the car since the couple left Nebraska and that she was hungry, thirsty and tired.

"She didn't appear to be hurt physically. Her face and hands showed no indications that she had been hit or harmed in any way.

"As I understand it the girl is now in Converse County Hospital in Douglas," Romer said.

— *Journal, Jan. 30, 1958*

On Thursday, both Charles Starkweather and Caril Fugate waived extradition to Nebraska; Wyoming did not object. Wyoming's governor, an opponent of capital punishment who had commuted three previous death sentences and had said he would commute Starkweather's if the youth were found guilty in Wyoming, signed the extradition. Nebraska lawmen who had flown to Wyoming in an Air National Guard plane decided to return the teen-agers to Lincoln by car after both said they did not wish to fly.

In the car that first day, Starkweather confessed to Lancaster County Sheriff Merle Karnopp that he had killed Lincoln service station attendant Robert Colvert on Dec. 1. There were other details in The Star's main story Friday morning from Gering, where the cars carrying the accused slayers stopped overnight at the Scotts Bluff County jail:

Youth's Oral Confession Solves Dec. 1 Murder

GERING, Neb. — Nineteen-year-old Charles Starkweather of Lincoln, who admittedly shot, knifed and clubbed 10 victims to death on a murderous rampage which ended Wednesday, orally confessed his eleventh slaying Thursday night, the Dec. 1 killing of Lincoln service station attendant Robert Colvert, Lancaster County Sheriff Merle Karnopp said.

Karnopp said the youth admitted all 11 murders while en route from Douglas, Wyo., to Gering, where he and his 14-year-old companion, Caril Fugate, are being held overnight.

Karnopp quoted Starkweather as saying, "I always wanted to be a criminal but not this big a one." The sheriff said the youth told him he "wasn't mad at anyone," but "just wanted to be somebody."

The youth showed no sign of remorse during the trip, Karnopp said.

The sheriff said Starkweather talked freely and cool as a cucumber as they rode in the back seat of one of the two cars making up the caravan.

"I have never seen a more vicious mad killer who could talk so cool and collected," said Karnopp. Starkweather, he said, declared he had a hatred that just built up inside himself.

Karnopp said Starkweather had little to say about Caril except that she had no part in the slayings.

The Lincoln law officer said Starkweather, in relating the Lincoln filling station attendant slaying, declared he hadn't meant to kill anybody when he entered the station bent on robbery.

Starkweather said he forced the attendant, Robert Colvert, into a car at gun point and drove into the country.

Karnopp said Starkweather related he was wearing a handkerchief over his face and that Colvert grabbed for it and Starkweather killed him.

Karnopp said he asked Starkweather why the three family members of Caril's family, Marion Bartlett, his wife, Velda, and their two-year-old daughter, had been killed and Starkweather replied he "argued with Bartlett." Beyond that Starkweather would say little, Karnopp stated.

At the Scotts Bluff County jail Karnopp asked Starkweather if he was tired and wanted to get a good sleep. He said Starkweather replied, "I slept like a log last night."

Starkweather had a meal of scrambled eggs and bacon before he went to bed Thursday night.

A doctor was called in to see if Caril needed any medical attention and she, too, had a meal of eggs and bacon.

The pony-tailed 14-year-old was given a sedative by a Gering physician and lodged in a separate — and less sturdy — cell.

Starkweather's 11th confession Thursday night — that of what was the first of his ugly admitted slayings — apparently closed the lid on the investigation into the Colvert case.

The 21-year-old attendant had been on night duty at the Crest Service Station on Cornhusker Highway.

Information had been developed this week that Starkweather borrowed the shotgun of his brother, Rodney, several days before Colvert's death and returned the weapon a day or so afterwards, according to Lincoln officials.

Also, it has been disclosed that the redhead was acquainted with Colvert and "had slept a number of times at the service station."

Colvert's body was found on a county road north of Lincoln Dec. 1. He had been shot in the head and robbed of some $160 in station receipts.

His expectant wife was among the survivors.

— *Star, Jan. 31, 1958*

Lincoln police were quick to voice their doubts of Caril's story:

Police Doubt Caril

Lincoln police expressed grave doubts Thursday about Caril Fugate's story that she was held hostage for eight days by Charles Starkweather.

Chief Joe Carroll said several times during the eight days she had ample opportunity to get away from Starkweather, according to incidents reported to police.

The girl's story that her parents, Mr. and Mrs. Marion Bartlett and her little half-sister, Betty Jean, were killed 10 days ago was also doubted.

Chief Carroll said he had reports that the family was seen buying groceries two days later than that.

Starkweather, however, according to Lincoln detective Lt. Eugene Henninger in Douglas, Wyo., also claims that the Bartletts were killed a week ago Tuesday.

Statements by Caril also implicated Starkweather in the Dec. 1 slaying of service station attendant Robert Colvert. She named another youth as the actual killer.

A check on the other youth, Chief Carroll said, revealed that he had not been in Lincoln for almost a year.

Caril also said a gang of youths had headquartered at the dead Bartletts' home in Belmont for several days while plotting to rob a bank.

The girl's statement added that the other boys "chickened out" after a time and departed.

The chief said police here had received little information from Wyoming on the bank robbery angle but were doing what they could with available leads.

Employees of a Lincoln bank said they were sure they had seen Starkweather hanging around the bank, but an official pointed out that garbage haulers often waited in the bank doorway before going to work. Starkweather was a garbage hauler until fired recently.

Pointing to these and other loose ends in the fantastic chain of deaths, the chief said there would be no relaxing of the investigation into any of the dozens of unanswered questions.

— *Star, Jan. 31, 1958*

Thus began an argument about Caril's role that was never to be definitively settled.

NEWER NEWS TAKES OVER

Friday, Jan. 31, found Lincoln quieter than it had been in days. But the Starkweather case continued to consume huge amounts of the space in the Lincoln newspapers, and staffs of both papers continued to develop stories on various aspects of the case. By Friday, many members of both staffs already had worked far past the usual 40 hours for the week. The Journal devoted more than 80 percent of its front page to the case in its city edition Friday, with two major developments: continuing colorful statements to law enforcement officers by Starkweather as he was enroute back to Lincoln under heavy guard, and initial comments on various aspects of police handling of the case.

Starkweather's comments came in a United Press story from Gering, Nebraska, quoting Lancaster County Sheriff Merle Karnopp:

Starkweather Details Murder Spree

GERING — Accused killer Charles Starkweather has admitted murdering 11 persons in two states because of a "hatred that built up in me," authorities said.

"Since I was a child I wanted to be an outlaw, but I didn't want it to go this far," the 19-year-old Lincolnite told authorities.

Sheriff Merle Karnopp said Starkweather made the statements during their trip by car from Douglas, Wyo., to Gering.

Starkweather, and his teenage companion, Caril Fugate, left Gering at 10:42 a.m. (CST) Friday for a 420-mile automobile trip to Lincoln, where the pair will face formal murder charges.

Starkweather, still wearing the blood-stained shirt he had on when captured Wednesday near Douglas, Wyo., and wearing glasses, was handcuffed and was wearing a heavy restraining belt, which kept his arms low.

The fugitives were in separate cars, each with three officers. One car was driven by a Lancaster County deputy sheriff, the other by Leo Knutson of the Patrol's criminal division in Scottsbluff. The Fugate girl was attended by Mrs. Merle Karnopp, wife of the Lancaster County sheriff.

Karnopp, who took personal custody of Starkweather, said his stocky prisoner was happy to be en route.

"I want to go back to Nebraska because Wyoming has a gas chamber and I don't like the smell of gas," Starkweather was quoted by the sheriff. "I suppose they'll have the chair ready for me."

Karnopp said that besides admitting the nine killings in the Lincoln area and one in Wyoming during his five-day murder rampage, Starkweather also confessed the slaying of a Lincoln service station attendant last Dec. 1.

Starkweather admitted he forced the attendant, Robert Colvert, 21, into his car the night of the slaying and drove out to a desolate country road, where he blasted the victim in the head with a shotgun and robbed him of about $80, the sheriff said.

Apparently the murder preyed on his mind and he turned on Caril's family in a blind rage because they resented his going with their daughter.

Last Saturday, the mass murder rampage began with the killing of Caril's mother, Mrs. Velda M. Bartlett, 36, and her stepfather, Marion Bartlett, 57, with bullets in the head, and budgeoning to death of the Bartletts' daughter, Betty Jean, 2.

Starkweather then held Caril hostage in the Bartlett home until Monday when Caril's grandmother became suspicious and notified police.

They fled to near Bennet, where Starkweather's car became stuck in the snow and a teenage couple Robert Jensen, 17, and Carol King, 16, both of Bennet, picked him up.

Starkweather told the sheriff he marched the two at gunpoint to a storm cellar in an abandoned school yard and ordered the boy into the cellar, killing Jensen when the boy tried to escape.

Then he shot Miss King at the cellar entrance and threw her in, the sheriff said. Starkweather denied that he committed an unnatural sex act with Miss King although pathologists said the girl had been a victim of such an attack.

The sheriff said Starkweather confessed he killed August Meyer, 70, a bachelor farmer of near Bennet, when Meyer came to the door of his home later Monday night with a gun in his hand. Starkweather said he assumed Meyer had heard him about him and was prepared to defend himself. Meyer was shot and killed as he stood in the doorway of his home.

On Tuesday night, Starkweather invaded the fashionable Lincoln home of C. Lauer Ward, 48, at random, the sheriff said. Starkweather shot Ward, president of Capital Steel Works of Lincoln, and fatally stabbed Ward's wife, Clara, 46, and their maid, Lillian Fencl, 51, the sheriff quoted the young slayer.

Starkweather and Caril have been formally charged with the murder of Miss King. Caril, who told authorities Starkweather planned to kill her "when we got to Washington," still was pale and shaken when she arrived at the Scotts Bluff County jail here.

Douglas Sheriff Earl Heflin, with whom Caril rode, said she sat silently during the trip last night.

Mrs. Steve Warrick, wife of the Scotts Bluff County sheriff, told newsmen she talked with Caril this morning and said the girl told her she did not know her parents, Mr. and Mrs. Marion Bartlett, had been killed. She told Mrs. Warrick she remembered that Starkweather had threatened to kill them if they did not permit her to go with him.

Mrs. Warrick, who said the girl seemed in a state of shock, said

Lancaster County Sheriff Merle Karnopp picked up Starkweather in Wyoming.

Caril told her that Starkweather "made me stay in the car" when he accosted Robert Jensen, 17, and Carol King, 16, of Bennet and killed them. She said she was in the car when he marched them to an abandoned school yard and shot them down.

— Journal, Jan. 31, 1958

Another key Starkweather comment came in a brief story from North Platte, where Starkweather was allowed out of the car for some exercise:

NORTH PLATTE — Accused slayer Charles R. Starkweather said he did not force 14-year-old Caril Ann Fugate to accompany him during the time in which he says he killed 10 persons.

He said he was with her at the Marion Bartlett home last weekend when relatives tried to enter the house but he added that he "didn't hold a gun on her or tell her what to say."

"Starkweather . . . said 'she could have got away but didn't try' during their trip from Lincoln to Douglas, Wyo."

Lincoln Police Lt. Eugene Robert Henninger said she (Caril Fugate) talked frequently with Mrs. Karnopp and "seemed to be angrier all the time at Chuck." He said she "still claimed she was a bystander" during the 10 murders.

— Journal, Jan. 31

Meanwhile, the top story in the Journal that day was one about the Colvert murder, in which a service station attendant had been slain almost two months before the latest murder spree. The Journal took the unusual step of copyrighting a story by Del Snodgrass and Leo Scherer that was headlined in a double banner across the top of the page: "4 Say They Gave Tips in December Linking Starkweather to Colvert Case."

That story reported: "At least four Lincolnites say they gave law enforcement officials the name of Charles Starkweather and the description of his car early in December in connection with the Dec. 1 killing of Robert Colvert." The story listed four people who had given descriptions of Starkweather, but the details recited in the body of the story did not include any case of Starkweather's name having been given to police at that point.

The authors of the story were to continue to write many stories on the case for the Journal, with Snodgrass reporting the case through both of the trials that followed.

Accompanying the story on page one were stories about a police review of all the murders, ordered by Mayor Bennett Martin, who asked for "a report in writing from Chief of Police Joe Carroll and Safety Director Emmett Junge." The front page also featured official comments on police actions and on their lack of manpower.

For the Journal, it had been a hectic week as the story developed during the hours in which the paper was going to press. City editor Neale Copple remembers that sometime later he was asked, for an article in a national professional magazine, how the Journal had "sensationalized" its coverage that week. Copple's reply was that it had been impossible to sensationalize the story, that just relating the facts had provided a real horror story.

The Star's top story on the case in Saturday morning's paper also dealt with descriptions of Starkweather given in the Colvert case, but it pointed out that while the description was given, no name had been mentioned.

Below a picture of Starkweather being escorted into the Nebraska State Penitentiary, The Star reported:

Admitted Slayer Returns To City

Nineteen-year-old Charles Starkweather, confessed killer of 11 persons, arrived in Lincoln Friday and was taken to the State Penitentiary for safekeeping.

Starkweather walked into the Penitentiary at 6:45 p.m. escorted by Lancaster County Sheriff Merle Karnopp. The 19-year-old admitted killer ignored pleas by some of the newsmen present to hold his head up for photographers.

He was taken immediately to a downstairs check-in room where he was relieved of his prized dark blue and white cowboy boots. Starkweather also turned in the black leather jacket, white shirt and black dungarees he has worn since at least Wednesday.

Prison officials issued him a pair of blue dungarees (without a belt), a blue chambray shirt and stringless loafers. He emerged from the check-in room 15 minutes after he had entered the prison and was escorted by guards to a cell in the institution's hospital ward.

Deputy Penitentiary Warden John Greenholz said Starkweather would occupy the same cell in which Lloyd Grandsinger was held for more than three years.

Grandsinger, convicted in 1954 of the shooting of a Safety Patrolman, is now in another part of the prison awaiting the outcome of a Nebraska appeal of a Federal District Court reversal of his conviction.

Greenholz said Starkweather would be "watched 24 hours a day." He will have no contact with other prisoners, and his stay will cost Lancaster County $4 a day.

His companion on the recent crime spree in which he admittedly killed 10 persons — 14-year-old Caril Fugate — waited outside in Karnopp's car with the sheriff's wife while her boyfriend was taken into the prison. She smiled and waved to photographers — her first such display since being taken into custody Wednesday — and had to be restrained when she tried to roll down the car window.

Caril was then driven to the Lancaster County Jail — where she ate a sandwich and drank a glass of milk — and was then taken to the Lincoln State Hospital for safekeeping. Due to her age she will

Gertrude Karnopp, wife of the sheriff (rear), escorts Fugate to her arraignment.

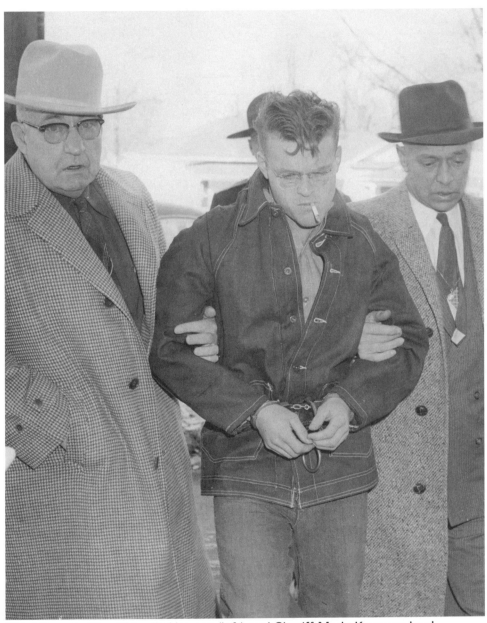

Chief Deputy Sheriff Leslie Hasson (left) and Sheriff Merle Karnopp lead Starkweather to his arraignment on murder charges.

not be held at the Penitentiary or county jail.

Indications were that County Attorney Elmer Scheele would take written statements from Starkweather and Caril Saturday.

It appears likely that neither Starkweather nor Caril will be arraigned until Monday on the first degree murder complaint filed against them in connection with the shooting of Carol King of Bennet.

— Star, Feb. 1, 1958

Altogether, the Journal devoted 68 columns of space to the Starkweather case that week. The Star devoted 59½ columns to the Starkweather story, with sometimes as little as half a column of other news on page one.

However, The Star's page one layout that Saturday morning took an interesting twist. City editor Earl Dyer had stayed late Thursday night to arrange for photographers and reporters to attend funeral services at several locations the next day for the victims of the killings, and he planned a photo layout for Saturday morning's front page that he felt would be a fitting end to the week: an eight-column panel of pictures under the somber headline: "Sorrowing County Buries Its Murdered Dead."

That layout of pictures and the stories on the funerals appeared on page two, not page one; in its place above the nameplate of the paper ran a story headlined: "U.S. Army Satellite Orbiting Earth." The story of the first U.S. satellite, long awaited in the space race with the Soviet Union, had replaced the Starkweather story as the top headline of the day. New news had inexorably pushed the old story to the inside pages.

LEFT: The bodies of Caril Fugate's mother, Velda Bartlett, 36, and her stepfather, Marion Bartlett, 58, were the first found. **ABOVE:** The Bartletts' baby daughter, Betty Jean, 2, also was found dead at their Belmont neighborhood home.

The victims and their killers

THE VICTIMS — SLUM TO COUNTRY CLUB

Of all the victims of the Starkweather murder spree, the least is known about those killed at the beginning of the week, the Bartletts, perhaps because they were people near the bottom rung of Lincoln's socio-economic ladder.

They lived in a poor section of the community, at 924 Belmont — a small, ramshackle five-room house covered with cheap imitation brick, its yard littered with debris. There were two dilapidated outbuildings, described in the newspapers as "sheds" — "a chicken house" or "small chicken coop," and "an abandoned outhouse" or "an outdoor toilet." There was no telephone; the bathroom was only a recent addition. Neighbors said Marion Bartlett and his wife were buying the home from its owners. A year after the murders, the owners filed a foreclosure action, alleging that $3,018 was due; the house was sold at auction.

Velda Bartlett, 37, was the mother, by a previous marriage, of Caril Fugate. She had another daughter, Barbara Von Busch, whose husband, Robert — together with Starkweather's brother Rodney — discovered the Bartlett bodies.

Marion Bartlett, 57, was a night watchman for Watson Bros. trucking firm in Lincoln. Days before the bodies were found, someone had called his company to say he was ill and would not report for work. The lack of a telephone at the Bartlett home explained why there was no further checking by the employer.

The Bartletts' own daughter, Betty Jean, would have been 3 years old on Feb. 11, 1958.

Nearly 50 relatives and friends attended their funeral, held at a mortuary. Mrs. Von Busch had been a member of the minister's church.

The next victim was August Meyer, whose body was found in an outbuilding behind his farm home near Bennet. Meyer was a bachelor, and his home was a typical older white frame farmhouse with a wide front porch.

Charles Starkweather had known Meyer previously. One story reported: "August's brother, Louis Meyer, who lived five miles northeast of Bennet, said the father of Charles Starkweather was in the habit of bringing his sons to the August Meyer place to hunt while the sons were boys.

"Last November, the Starkweather boys were out squirrel hunting on the place. They were in the habit of coming out every hunting season and knew the place well, Louis said.

"August always had been 'very nice' to the boys, Louis said."

Meyer left an estate that included $57,838 in cash, savings and checking accounts, bonds and insurance policies, as well as property he owned jointly with relatives, valued at $6,654. The value of his farm was not reported.

He was survived by his brother and three sisters. The story about his funeral referred to him as "well-liked."

Carol King, 16, and Robert Jensen, 17, were students in the junior class at Bennet High School, where Jensen was class president.

Carol King was survived by her mother, Mrs. Mabel King; a brother, Warren of Bennet; a sister, Mrs. LaVerne L. Stolte of Lincoln, and her grandfather, M.L. King of Bennet. Mabel King had just moved into Bennet, following the death of her husband Jan. 3, from the family farm near the town

There was much more publicity in the newspapers about Robert Jensen because it was with his murder that Charles Starkweather and Caril Fugate were charged. His mother was the author of a letter to the editor printed before Starkweather's trial:

In reply to "Wondering", March 6:

Your letter was well written and I agree with all of it. Our son was also brutally murdered.

We have already given up one son — a twin brother to our remaining son. This leaves our boy a lonely only child. Our son, Robert, had overcome polio, a serious eye injury, three sieges of pneumonia, a leg weakness, a broken nose, and a back injury suffered in football. At the time of his death he was recovering from a leg injury received in an auto accident while riding with a friend.

We had watched our son come through all those things with never a word of complaint, only concern for his loved ones who worried over him. He developed into a cheerful, loving young man who saw only the good in people.

Our grief is too personal and our loss is too great to be put into words, but this is a brief look at the kind of son and brother we had to give up.

MRS. ROBERT E. JENSEN
— *Star, March 10, 1958*

RIGHT: August Meyer, 70, was found dead in his rural Bennet farmhouse. **BELOW LEFT AND RIGHT:** The bodies of two Bennet teen-agers, Carol King, 16, and Robert Jensen, 17, were discovered in the storm cellar of a rural schoolhouse that had been razed.

Joint services for Carol King and Robert Jensen overflowed the Bennet Community Church. All businesses in the small town were closed, "even gas stations." Schools were dismissed for the afternoon.

The Wards were prominent and wealthy Lincolnites, a fact evidenced by their large home in the County Club section of the city and the fact that they had a housekeeper. C. Lauer Ward had met with Gov. Victor Anderson in the governor's statehouse office just the afternoon before his death. The Wards' relatives included some of Lincoln's most prominent families. An early story about the couple:

Ward Was Head of 2 Firms Here

C. Lauer Ward was president of both the Capital Bridge Co. and the Capital Steel Co. He and Mrs. Ward were active in a number of civic activities.

Mr. Ward was on the board of trustees of Bankers Life Insurance Co. of Nebraska and was a director of Provident Savings and Loan Association, Norden Labororatories and the National Bank of Commerce.

Mrs. Ward also was a graduate of the University of Nebraska and in 1952 was elected vice president of the Nebraska Alumni Assn., the highest position in which women serve in the Association.

Mr. Ward graduated from the University of Nebraska in 1932, attended Harvard Law School and the University of Chicago. He was a member of the Nebraska Bar Association, Sigma Alpha Epsilon and Phi Delta Phi legal fraternity.

Ward was a member of Rotary Club, and served on its board of directors.

Surviving the Wards are one son, Mike, 14, who attends Choate School at Wallingford, Conn.

Mrs. Ward has two sisters, Mrs. Phil Sidles of Lincoln and Mrs. Gilbert Reynolds of Grand Island, and a brother, Carl Olson of Lincoln. She also was an aunt of Bob Reynolds of Lincoln, former University of Nebraska football star.

She was a member of Delta Gamma sorority.

Dr. and Mrs. David Gracey, former Holy Trinity minister, called from Waterbury, Conn., to say he was bringing the Ward son, Mike, back to Lincoln.

— Journal, Jan. 29, 1958

The Wards' estate inventory listed a number of stockholdings, bonds and cash, and the estate paid state inheritance taxes totaling $229,994 on a valuation of more than $1 million. C. Lauer Ward's stock in Capital Bridge was valued at $557,980; his stock in Capital Steel was listed at $359,504.

Some 1,500 people attended the services for the Wards, held at Westmin-

ABOVE LEFT AND RIGHT: Clara Ward, 46, and her husband, C. Lauer Ward, 48, were found slain in their Country Club neighborhood home. **RIGHT:** Also found dead at the Ward home was their housekeeper, Lillian Fencl, 51.

Merle Collison, 37, was slain on a Wyoming highway.

Service station attendant Robert Colvert, 21, was the first victim.

ster Presbyterian Church because their own church, Holy Trinity Episcopal, had burned and had not yet been replaced.

The Wards' housekeeper, Lillian Fencl, was 51, and had been "with the Ward family for 26 years," having been employed by Mr. and Mrs. Chester Ward, parents of the slain man, and remained in the home after the elder Ward's death. At her funeral the minister noted that "Miss Fencl was treated as a member of the family," a phrase commonly used in those times to describe a valued, longtime servant. She was survived by her parents, of nearby Wahoo, Neb., and two sisters.

Merle Collison, a shoe salesman, was asleep in his 1956 Buick parked along the highway near Douglas, Wyo., when Starkweather came upon the car. Collison carried papers listing Great Falls, Mont., as his home town, but his car had an Oregon license plate. The Lincoln papers, busy with 10 victims in their own city, did not carry additional information on him.

The young man Starkweather admitted murdering nearly two months earlier was Robert George Colvert, 21, the night attendant at the Crest service station at 1545 Cornhusker Highway. Colvert had been employed there less than a month; he had been discharged from the Navy in October. He and his wife lived with his father; other survivors included a brother and four married sisters.

REDHEADED SWAGGERER

Starkweather — Five feet five inches tall, 140 pounds, scar over right eye, green eyes, dark red hair cut short on top, long on sides and in back, bowlegged and pigeon-toed, swaggers when he walks, believed wearing blue jeans and black leather motorcycle jacket, black boots or cowboy boots. Sometimes has speech impediment, trouble pronouncing Ws and Rs.

— Police description, Journal, Jan. 28, 1958

Charles Starkweather was not known publicly prior to Jan. 27, 1958. But within days he became the object of intense curiosity, and of a flurry of personality sketches and "background" pieces in the local newspapers.

Immediately after his capture, an International News Service report described him this way:

Dirty, Shaggy Starkweather Glumly Ponders Fate

Douglas, Wyo. — Charles Starkweather, a glum teenager facing charges of murdering his way through Nebraska and Wyoming, sat in his gray jail cell Wednesday night wondering what will happen next.

Starkweather, shaggy and wearing clothing stained with his own blood, looked older behind bars than he is — 19.

His hair, lacklustre and reddish-brown, curled unevenly about his neck and ears. The only sign of neatness about him was his gold-rimmed glasses that clung tightly to his nose with the lens close to his eyes.

His white shirt was ripped down the back and dirty around the collar. There was blood on the front of the shirt and on the shoulder — his own blood shed from the lobe of his right ear cut by flying glass during his bullet-punctured chase and capture near Douglas, Wyo.

Starkweather's blue jeans fit his chunky thighs snugly and when he stood and walked in his cell, his black oxford shoes fidgeted on the floor of the cell.

Converse County Sheriff Earl Heflin turned the photographers loose in the battleship-gray painted corridor of the jail at Douglas, and that's when Starkweather got nervous.

First he sat sullenly on the top bunk laced with an uncovered mattress. He smoked a cigarette and stared at his shadow thrown by the stacked lights of the photographers.

Then the youth eased down from the bunk and faced a wall. A moment later he looked out the small window on the far side of his cell to hide his face from the cameras and lights that kept blinking and winking at him.

Starkweather moved his body slowly and deliberately, some

what nervously, but not defiantly. His face contorted frequently at the far cell window as he bit his lip and rubbed his large jaw with the back of his hand.

Everywhere he glanced there was a face looking at him. He could have hidden by lying on a bottom bunk and turning his face to the corner of the cell.

But he didn't try to hide.

— Star, Jan. 30, 1958

Anyone who had known Starkweather and was willing to talk was quoted in the newspapers. One of the first was the manager of the apartment building in which Starkweather had a room:

Starkweather Behind On Rent, Unemployed

Mrs. May Hawley, of 425 No. 10th, expressed sentiments of Caril Fugate's relatives, that "we know that boy has forced Caril into this" and "we're expecting to hear at any minute that she's been found dead."

Mrs. Hawley, who manages the apartment building on No. 10th., said that Caril's family are living there, and that Charles Starkweather had been a tenant there "until last Tuesday when I told him he'd have to pay his back rent."

Mrs. Hawley said that 19-year-old Starkweather had lived at 425 No. 10th for about two months. She said he moved there after the youth had had an argument with his father over damage to the Starkweather car.

The woman explained that she had warned the youth to pay three weeks rent due her, and when he failed to, had padlocked the room. Starkweather had promised her to return last Saturday with the rent money. Saturday was the approximate date police said that the triple killing of Mr. and Mrs. Marion Bartlett and their daughter, Betty Jean, occurred. Starkweather never returned to pay his rent.

Orin Hawley, husband of the apartment manager, called Starkweather "a small fellow who never caused any trouble." He described the youth sought in connection with the slaying of the Bartlett family and three Bennet residents as short, bowlegged, and always wearing cowboy boots and a broad-brimmed hat.

— Journal, Jan. 29, 1958

One of the first articles painted a picture of a short, slight youth with poor eyesight and not enough "mind power" to "do more than just lift things around." That article, by the Journal's Marj Marlette, who later may have come to know Starkweather as well as anyone outside his family, sounded a note repeated many times later — that the young man had shown no advance sign that he could become a mass killer.

Disorders 'Not Manifested Before Murderous Rampage'

Lincoln, far away from metropolitan teen-age gang wars, has spawned a killer — a 19-year-old who bragged: "I shot 'em all" when finally captured.

What triggered his rampage?

Did anything in his earlier life indicate he was dangerous to society?

A slight, short youth, Charles Starkweather has an IQ slightly below average.

When he quit school at 16 he was emotionally insecure, nervous and had a speech difficulty.

Guns, shooting and hot-rods seem to have been his hobbies.

Surprisingly, though he was known as a crack shot (and is believed to have accurately killed nine of ten victims with a shot in the head), his eyesight had earlier been reported "poor."

Though now it is obvious his personality disorders were severe, they do not seem to have been manifested openly before his murder rampage.

He had no juvenile record, nor had he been sent to the school guidance office as a particular behavior problem.

John Hedge, manager of Western Newspaper Union, said Starkweather worked for him — "I think it was until last June" — and that Starkweather "never made enough of an impression on me so that I can even remember when he started to work."

Hedge said Starkweather caused no trouble, showed no fits of temper and always did what he was told. "We were all surprised around here when we learned he was in this trouble.

"I was going to turn him loose last summer. I wanted a man with more mind power who could do more than just lift things around. But I didn't have to fire him. He came in and said, 'I want to resign.' "

The employer continued: "Everybody was kind of sorry for him while he worked here because he was so weak minded."

As for spare time activities, Hedge said Starkweather was a hot rod fanatic and joined several other fellows in making a hot rod.

What explains Charles' actions — as nearly as any inconceivable actions can be explained?

Relatives of the sharp-shooting youth said he had a bad temper and once angry kept right on burning with his "mad."

In school, perhaps, was the only contact through which Charles' potentials could have been discovered.

Children recognized as maladjusted are sent to the school psychiatrist, diagnoses are made of their problems and plans made for their treatment by the Child Guidance Clinic or the University of Nebraska.

The actual treatment, however, depends on the parents — it

can't be forced unless some overt act of delinquency takes place and the child goes through juvenile court.

Charles, however, does not appear to have been recognized as that much of a problem.

And Police Chief Joe Carroll said Starkweather's only police record involved a "minor" violation last year when Charles was brought in for permitting a minor (Caril Fugate) to drive a car.

As for his home background, the youth came from a fairly large family who moved about town.

His father, a carpenter and cabinet maker, is now out of work. In 1950, while the father had a bad back, the family received help from welfare sources but is not now getting any help.

Both the father, Guy, and the mother, Helen Arnold, are native Nebraskans — born at Table Rock and Palmyra, respectively.

Guy Starkweather claims that his son went "berserk" because "he faced blindness." (Criminologist Reinhardt observed: "If that is an excuse for wholesale killing, think of the people who'd be committing murders.")

A Lincoln optometrist, Dr. Leonard Fitch, said he fitted Starkweather with glasses July 24, 1954. Starkweather was myopic and vision without glasses was poor although nothing was unusual about the case.

Without glasses, Starkweather tested 20-200 (anything poorer than this, if not correctible, is regarded as blindness under Nebraska law, making an individual eligible for blind assistance). Glasses corrected his vision to 20-30. Dr. Fitch said he had no record of subsequent examinations.

The father also said that Charles was worried because he'd lost several jobs, had recently suffered illness that caused him to lose 30 pounds, and a few years ago had been hit on the forehead with a 2-by-4 and "had never felt right since."

"All of this just built up inside of him until he went berserk," the father said.

Recently, Charles was fired as a garbage collector because, his own brother said, he was too lazy to work.

And he left home six months ago after an argument over letting Caril Fugate drive the car.

— Journal, Jan. 30, 1958

During Starkweather's trial, the defendant bridled at comments being made about him:

Starkweather Wants 'Own Side' Told

Charles Starkweather asked his mother to "find a reporter" during court Wednesday "to tell his side" of his employment at the Western Newspaper Union.

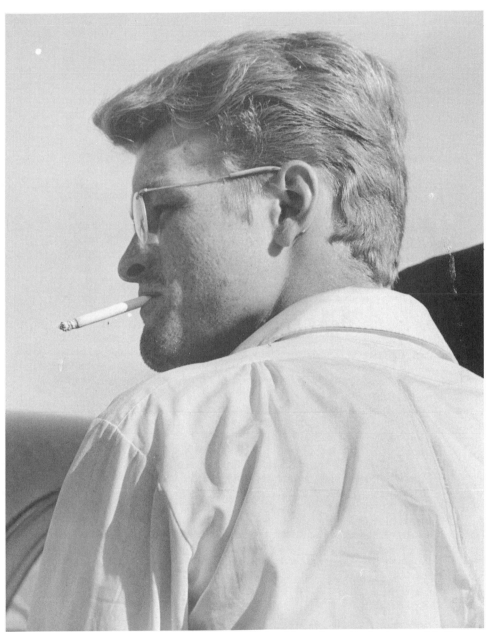

Starkweather frequently was photographed with a cigarette between his lips.

The request was made during a whispered conversation with his mother during the morning session as the company manager, John Hedge, testified that Charles "was the dumbest man who was working for us" of 12 or 13 warehousemen.

Hedge also termed Starkweather "mentally retarded" and an employee "you sometimes had to tell the same thing to 2 or 3 times."

Of Charles' resignation from his job of unloading trucks and baling papers, Hedge said: "He only sat and looked at me for a long time, and finally said 'I want to resign.' He must have sat there 2 or 3 minutes before saying anything."

Mrs. Starkweather, herself upset over the line of questioning by the defense to prove her son abnormal, spoke of Charles' worry "that the family will suffer from this."

Charles told his mother that he "was the only guy down there that had the nerve to quit."

Mrs. Starkweather also related that her son wanted it known that he quit because the management kept hiring "college boys whom Charlie had to train to use the machinery like the 'horse' (lifting or pulley) and then they (the new employees) would get ahead, and earn more than he did."

She also told of Charles' statement that "all the guys at the place felt the same way" about this situation.

"It just isn't fair of them," she said, referring to the defense attorneys who questioned the witnesses Wednesday on Charles' lack of intelligence and odd or unusual behavior. "I know I shouldn't but I thank Mr. Scheele in my heart when he shows that Charlie wasn't that bad," she added, referring to Co. Atty. Elmer Scheele's cross-examination of the defense witnesses.

She explained the defense attorneys told her they "didn't care whose toes they stepped on" in trying to save Starkweather from the electric chair.

As other family members took the stand Wednesday in Charles' defense, their manner showed they were unwilling to be led into saying anything derogatory against the youth on trial for his life.

The final defense witness Wednesday, Mrs. John Neal, who is Charles Starkweather's step-mother, finally broke into tears after repeated examination and cross-examination on whether Charles' demeanor had changed at all after the December 1 slaying of Robert Colvert.

Mrs. Neal called the defendant "always a good boy, a nice boy, happy and cheerful" and said she had noticed no change in his manner, later, even when she visited him at the State Penitentiary in April or May.

— Star, May 15, 1958

Charles Starkweather's IQ was a subject of continued comment — from the first days through the trial. At the trial, a school official testified:

Starkweather's IQ Rated Him Low Average

Charles Starkweather got good school reports in citizenship, according to testimony in his Lancaster District Court trial.

Otherwise, the murder defendant's scholastic achievements put him in the "lower ½ of his class" and intelligence tests generally rated him from "dull normal" to "low average."

Julius Humann, director of guidance for the Lincoln Public Schools, traced Starkweather's school career on subpoena of the defense.

Starkweather's citizenship grades in junior high were "above the average," Humann said on cross examination.

They included a 2 and 3 in the 7th grade; 1 and 3 in the 8th grade and two "goods" in the 9th grade, Humann read from the school records. (1 is the highest given; 7 the lowest, but grades below 4 in citizenship are seldom used, he explained.)

On questioning by the defense, Humann said that on a full-scale intelligence test given by a psychologist in 1954, Starkweather received an overall IQ rating of 91 — considered low average. (90 to 110 is considered average.)

Other tests administered in various grades by classroom teachers gave Starkweather IQs ranging from 86 or 87 — "dull normal" — except for one in the 70s — "borderline deficiency" — in 1951.

Humann explained that IQ tests may vary from time to time, and on a particular day — because of illness, etc. — may be lower, but never higher than a person's ability.

In his opinion statement to the jury, Defense Atty. T. Clement Gaughan had said that the defense would show Starkweather was "only a point or two above an idiot."

The "idiot" classification, however, is the lowest on the IQ range — 0 to 20. Anyone below 70 is considered of inferior intelligence, with 70 to 80 "borderline deficiency," Humann explained after court.

In junior high classes, Charles appeared to do best in drafting, woodwork, art, physical education and handicraft, getting 3s and 4s in these subjects. (The grading scale ranges from a high of 1 to a failing of 7.)

He flunked science in the eighth grade, and barely passed — with 6s — arithmetic in both the 7th and 8th grades.

In the 9th grade he was placed in a special class for slow learners though, Humann said, his total intelligence rating was actually too high for this class.

Starting school at Saratoga at 5, records show Charles received low average grades in the 1st, 2nd, 4th and 5th grades. He repeated the 3rd grade twice, then went into the 4th on "special adjustment" — since he was older than others and it was thought unwise to retain him for a third year in the same grade.

He also entered junior high at Irving, as a "special adjustment" pupil.

Attending Irving for 2 years and Everett for 1, Starkweather quit school after the 9th grade, Humann said.

— *Journal, May 15, 1958*

Lincolnites who had known the murder suspect in his youth also were interviewed:

Close Associates Recall Teenagers' Short Past;
Starkweather Was 'Daredevil' Hotrod Driver At Race Track

A background to the picture of two Lincoln teenagers involved in an unbelievable killing spree began to unfold as Lincolnites who had known them again talked in normal tones about the pair.

Much of the talk of past associates did not jibe with the picture of two frightened youths at the end of a "hide and kill" game with law officials.

Charles Starkweather, seemingly calm after his capture, first greeted Wyoming patrolmen with screams of "I'd kill you if I had a gun." Disheveled and sobbing over his superficial wounds, Starkweather nevertheless took time to light up the ever-present cigarette.

Yet, this boy who Wyoming law officers said "turned yellow" when he saw his own blood, was known as a "daredevil" by hotrod drivers at the Capital Speedways in Lincoln.

Jack Singer, Capital Speedways official, told of Chuck's "hanging around the track, although he never owned his own racer."

The "demolition derby" was Starkweather's meat. The "derby" features near-wrecked cars going in both directions around the narrow oval and meeting in head-on and rear collisions.

Chuck was considered as dangerous in these races because "he did almost anything," Singer recalled.

Retired principal of Everett Junior High, Mrs. Ruth Place, showed insight into Starkweather's personality as she said of her former pupil: "I think Charles wanted very badly to be somebody."

Parents and former classmates of 19-year-old Charles fill in other data:

He smokes too much.

He's a pretty good mechanic but didn't stick with any job he started.

He carries a knife much of the time, but usually fights with his fists.

He was called "Little Red" and "Big Red," both of which he disliked.

He "doesn't carry a grudge" but "gets mad fast."

He dated and "went steady" with several girls during the last five years.

A former girl friend of Starkweather's, who asked that her name not be made known, said this about the youth whom she knew four years ago in ninth grade:

"I felt sorry for Charles because everyone else shunned him.

"He is a red head and bowlegged and people inclined to push him around. They always gave Chuck a bad deal.

"I met him after he was kicked out of Irving (Junior High School). Nobody would accept him.

"We went to the movies together and spent a lot of evenings at home studying.

"In all the time I knew him I never once heard him swear and he never smoked or drank. He never even tried to put his arm around me. He went to some of my church affairs with me and even ran errands for my mother.

"I think he was one of the finest boys I've ever known.

"I can't believe he's done this. Maybe he's changed a lot in the last four years. Maybe I shouldn't pity him, but I think more people should have given him a chance."

— Star, Jan. 31, 1958

But the richest source of information was Charles Starkweather's own family.

His father, Guy, an unemployed carpenter, was quoted on Wednesday when the youth was still at large as saying, "It's a terrible thing to have to lock the windows and doors of your own house against your own son.

"I trusted Charlie and thought I could talk with him until he killed the old man (August Meyer). But if he'll kill an old friend like August, he'll turn on his own father," he told a Journal reporter. The elder Starkweather went on: "It could have been a lot of things. He has lost a couple of good jobs, that girl (Caril Fugate) has him wrapped around her finger, he is to lose his sight within a year and a recent cold made him lose 30 pounds and he may still be sick and delirious. Then a few years ago he got hit on the forehead with a 2-by-4."

Starkweather's mother, Helen, wept that day as she told the Journal reporter: "Chuck is no better than anyone else who has killed."

Mrs. Starkweather, a waitress, was less willing than her husband to talk about her son, but she related that Rodney (another son) once "told us something that scared me a little bit.

"He said that when he and Chuck went hunting and Chuck was using an automatic rifle, he could not quit shooting once he started to pull the trigger.

"He would shoot crazy-like and empty the gun at no target at all."

Later, during Charles' trial, she told a reporter her children helped at home: "Charles can wash and iron as well as I can," she said.

Starkweather's parents, Helen and Guy, pose with another son, Rodney.

An interview with Charles' brother Rodney reported:

Charlie Always Was Tough — But Murder?

Rodney Starkweather, the shocked brother of a youth sought by law authorities, tried to realize what had happened.

The 21-year-old garbage and trash hauler sat in his two-room apartment with his pregnant wife, trying to figure out what could have prompted his 19-year-old brother, Charles, to be sought for questioning in connection with six slayings.

"Charlie always was tough," Rodney added. "He knew how to handle himself. He once gave me a cauliflower ear. But murder? Oh, God, I just don't know."

Charles Starkweather and Caril Fugate, 14, were being sought in seven states for questioning in connection with the slaying of Caril's mother, her stepfather, her half-sister, two teenagers from a nearby community and an elderly farmer.

"Charlie always loved to fight," Rodney said of his red-haired brother. "He really has a temper."

However, Rodney said that he had noticed "how all those people were shot in the head" and added:

"Charlie was a good shot. When we'd go hunting, the game he shot was always shot right in the head."

The older brother said Charles was "booted out" of one junior high school and didn't go to school after his graduation from the ninth grade.

Rodney said Charles was always interested in mechanics and had once owned a stock car that he raced at a local track. He said "all his money went into his cars — he talked about building another car, but he never got around to it."

Rodney said his brother "always had a tough life."

"There are seven of us kids — Gregg, 7; David, 13, Bob, 15, Lavetta, 16; Charlie, me and Leonard is a chef in Washington."

— *Journal, Jan. 29, 1958*

The question of whether Charles Starkweather was insane was to come up time and again during his trial, but the jury's ultimate decision was that he was sane. One of the poignant moments in the trial occurred when Helen Starkweather, asked if her son was mentally deficient or insane, responded, "You have no right to ask a mother something like that."

Of that day's testimony, The Star reported:

Sitting directly facing her son during his testimony and smiling encouragement was Helen Starkweather. Her smiles went unheeded by the youth.

Earlier Mrs. Starkweather had been seated stiffly in the same witness chair, telling that "Charles had been a changed boy" since he had met Caril Fugate.

"He told me he was sorry for all this," she defended her son, and later explained under cross examination that Charles had told her he "didn't wake up and realize what he had done until later."

The frail young woman, near tears at times during her 40 minutes on the stand, stood firm against the defense attempt to make her admit that her son might be mentally deficient or insane.

"I refuse to answer!" she snapped. "I'm his mother. You have no right to ask a mother something like that." And her son's attorneys turned their questions in other directions.

— *Star, May 16, 1958*

Mrs. Starkweather also objected to defense attempts to portray her son as showing "lack of remorse," quoting a letter he wrote in the Wyoming jail: "There, he says he is sorry. And he shows he is worried about the family."

Mrs. Starkweather at one point was quoted as saying of her children that she had raised "six problems and one catastrophe." Later, after she had seen the statement in print and there had been public comment on it, she telephoned The Star to dictate this letter:

Killer's Mother Speaks

Editor's Note: Mrs. Guy Starkweather, mother of Charles Starkweather, called The Star Friday night and asked if she could give an open letter to the people of Lincoln. The Star here presents the letter, just as it was dictated by Mrs. Starkweather.

————

To the interested parties in Lincoln:

I have heard there has been comments on my statement of my "six problems and one catastrophe." I will admit that what happened to Charles in that week was a catastrophe. Few can deny that.

I did not mean that I had raised six problems in the definition the dictionary gives to the word "problem." What I meant was, I had problems to be met. Every mother and father has.

Each child at some time or other has a different problem and has come to me and his father for a solution. Sometimes the answer we gave was the same as far as the other children, sometimes different, according to how we felt we could best get the answer across to the child's understanding.

At the pace this old world is set today, one cannot deny there are numerous problems that children and youth find hard to cope with. What with the atomic bomb, the speed of our planes being faster than sound, Sputnik, and our world is coming to, so we should see what our young folks are up against.

Do you parents believe that you can always give an answer to your chidren and know that they have fully grasped the meaning? I don't think so.

Every mother and father knows that each child is a separate individual, each with different ideas and thoughts. We love each and every one of our children, one no more than the other.

There are problems for a parent to meet in the years of raising a family, sometimes small, other times large. We have taught our children that when they come up against something they do not understand not to dodge it but to face it to the best of their ability.

I think all of us at some time in our lives, probably mostly in younger years, met with something that was really an obstacle, but with the help and understanding of our parents we surmounted that obstacle and were better persons because of it. When one of my children came to me with a problem and were seeking the best explanation I could give I hoped they understood. My problem was, did they?

Anything that needs thinking and working out is a problem,

mathematics, or diagramming a sentence for an English lesson.

That is what I meant by "six problems and a catastrophe." We all have a big problem on our hands sometimes in trying to understand our children. I truly hope everyone understands what I am trying to get across. I thank you all very much.

Mrs. Guy Starkweather
— *Star, May 17, 1958*

Charles' father, Guy, couldn't be found at the trial and was reported to be unwilling to take the stand. He testified at the trial only after being subpoenaed:

Starkweather's Father: 'Charlie Didn't Use Good Judgment'

"Well, I don't think he used good judgment, no," Guy Starkweather commented on his son's murder spree activities.

This gross understatement was the elder Starkweather's only comment to his son's attorneys' attempt to show his son was insane.

"He ain't never done anything crazy to me," said Guy Starkweather about his son's attitude, but he added that "a man can do a lot of things if he's scared enough and on the run."

The attempts of T. Clement Gaughan to make Guy Starkweather label his son "insane" led to an exchange between the two when Gaughan asked:

"And after what he is alleged to have done, after what he told you he did, can you say he is perfectly normal?"

Starkweather retorted quickly, "Does he act insane now?"

And Gaughan fired back, "Well, can anyone be normal who goes to sleep while his confessions are being read?"

But the elder Starkweather had an explanation: "He heard them plenty times before."

Charles Starkweather had apparently been dozing while Gaughan sat in the witness chair reading a series of confessions on the 12 killings in which the 19-year-old had been involved.

The fight that preceded Charles' leaving home was described several times by Guy Starkweather during his testimony under oath.

"We never had a big fight," Guy Starkweather said. "That time in September, he slipped and stumbled and went through the window," he related, explaining the outcome of his argument with his son over allowing 14-year-old Caril Fugate to drive the Starkweather car. "It was pretty close quarters in there," he explained.

Later he said, about the same fight, "Charlie slapped at me and I slapped back," and added that he fought with his son "just that once."

He admitted under further questioning that the fight started

when "he got sassy, and I made the first pass and he hit me back."
About Caril Fugate, Mr. Starkweather was willing to admit that as
his son's interest in the teenager grew, "Charlie more or less
seemed different."

But he added, unprompted by a question, "Miss Fugate always
seemed to me like a pretty nice little lady, until this."

And what would it mean to the Starkweather family if Charles is
found insane, Guy Starkweather was asked.

"I guess we can take that along with the rest of it," the elder
Starkweather said, shaking his head.

— Star, May 17, 1958

Starkweather family members all declined to say their son and brother was
insane. Eventually, the jury agreed with them.

A Journal story by Marj Marlette near the end of the trial summed up testimony about Charles' personality:

3 Personality Pictures Drawn

Charles Starkweather, who went into his murder trial an unknown quantity, has emerged from psychiatric testimony as three
possible personalities.

One appears legally sane, one legally insane, and one a part of
each.

The different faces of Charles presented to the jury — which
must determine his sanity — include the following:

A man of no feeling and understanding, an animal rather than a
human being. (Insane, acording to the defense testimony of psychologist Nathan Greenbaum and Dr. John O'Hearne of Kansas
City.)

A man with a personality defect, with immature feeling, but who
knew what he was doing and who uses a brash front to cover his
true feeling. (Sane, according to the state's testimony of Dr. Robert Stein, Dr. Edwin Coats, and psychologist Charles Munson, all
of Lincoln.)

Or a man who had some feelings and might ordinarily act rea-
sonably, but who, under stress, did not know right from wrong or
the consequences of his action. (Possibly insane at the time of his
crime, as indicated psychiatrist John Steinman of Lincoln.)

Which person Charles is — a man of no feelings, a man who
covers them up cockily — no one may ever know for sure.

But the jury will determine whether he is sane or insane.

— Journal, May 22, 1958

Mrs. Starkweather took pains to write to the press and talk to reporters to
make her points public. Then, almost a year later, appeared a final, polite letter
from her:

Grateful

Lincoln — We are grateful to the Pardon Board for its consideration in granting a hearing for Charles Starkweather and extending his execution and extend our thanks to the prison officials for their help to Charles in making his application for the hearing.

We know that the state is a minister of God revenger to execute wrath upon him that doeth evil. In view of this we are asking the Board to review Charles' case and take all facts into consideration in the question of commuting his sentence.

GUY and HELEN STARKWEATHER
— *Journal, March 5, 1959*

Helen Starkweather filed for divorce from Guy in June 1961, on grounds of extreme cruelty.

WHAT KIND OF GIRL?

Caril Fugate — Five feet one inch tall, 105 pounds, looks about 18, blue eyes, dark brown hair usually worn in pony tail, sometimes wears glasses, possibly wearing ring with red setting, dressed in jeans and blouse or sweater, may be wearing a medium blue parka. Might have on white baton boots or gray suede loafers.

— Police description, Journal, Jan. 29, 1958

What kind of girl was Caril Fugate? That's a question asked many times and never answered conclusively. There were those who thought they had the answer, but no one could prove his or her version was correct.

The Lincoln newspapers began asking the question early, only a day after Caril Fugate's mother, stepfather and stepsister had been found murdered. One of the first to talk to reporters was a landlady:

Youth's Ex-Landlady Sure Girl Wasn't His Willing Accomplice

Mrs. May Hawley, of 425 No. 10th, expressed sentiments of Caril Fugate's relatives, that "we know that boy has forced Caril into this" and "we're expected to hear at any minute that she's been found dead."

Mrs. Hawley, who manages the apartment building on No. 10th, said that Caril's family had lived there, and that Charles Starkweather had been a tenant there "until last Tuesday when I told him he'd have to pay his back rent."

(Orin) Hawley said that Caril was a frequent visitor at the No. 10th apartment and always visited with his wife. He explained that Caril and her mother, the slain Mrs. Velda Fugate Bartlett, lived at the No. 10th apartments for several years before the mother's marriage to Marion Bartlett.

Mrs. Hawley called Caril "an awfully good girl who never could have done anything like this" and said that Caril had been attending Whittier Junior High School. Caril drove to the school almost daily in the Starkweather car, Mrs. Hawley said. "I don't believe she was old enough to have a license," Mrs. Hawley said.

"She always stopped in to see me and chat, but the boy (Starkweather) I never got to know very well. He seemed all right."

Hawley said that recently, ending when Starkweather was evicted, Caril visited the youth in his room almost every evening.

— Star, Jan. 29, 1958

Caril Fugate's father, William, and her mother had been divorced for several years, but her mother had legal custody of the teen-age girl. The day Starkweather and Caril were captured, William Fugate talked to a reporter for The Star:

Caril Fugate was 14 years old when she and Starkweather were arrested.

Father Insists Caril Traveled Under Force

A 14-year-old eighth-grader at Whittier Junior High School, who had her heart set on becoming a nurse, may never see her dream come true.

"I'm just tickled to death they got them," said William Fugate, father of Caril Ann, "and I'm thankful that she's safe."

Fugate continued:

"She's went through an awful lot the past few days. I just know she's been on the road all along against her will.

"She loved that little baby (the slain Bartlett baby) just like it was an angel. She always wanted to be a nurse.

"I know Caril Ann was held by guns. I just know she was, 'cause she wouldn't do it on her own free will. I wish she had quit going with Chuck. I never could see him anyway."

Fugate recalled the time when Caril was struck by an auto as she was crossing a street near Memorial Stadium:

"It happened on a Saturday. She was taken to the hospital and on Sunday she got up and went to church. She couldn't sit up and had to be taken home, but she was determined to go to church and nothing could have kept her home."

"Caril had been going with Chuck about one year," he said. "It must have been about two weeks ago that Betty (the slain Mrs. Bartlett and Fugate's ex-wife) told Charles to go away and not to come back," Fugate pointed out. "She also told him to stay away from Caril," he added.

Fugate added:

"We thought maybe he might be coming here to the apartment (1136½ K). I had a .410 gauge shotgun loaded and ready. I'd a stopped him one way or another."

Fugate described his daughter, who was an avid movie goer and comic book reader, as being able to carry a conversation and "talk a blue streak."

"I haven't slept for a long time. I've just been listening to the radio and sitting here hoping and praying for Caril's safety," the father said.

"She played it smart by sticking with him. If she comes out of this without a nervous breakdown, she'll be lucky," he said.

"Thank God they got him before he got any more. How could a man do those awful things?" he asked with an empty look.

— Star, Jan. 30, 1958

The girl's grandmother also stood behind her granddaughter in an interview with an Associated Press writer:

Caril's Grandmother: 'Prayer Is Only Hope'

"God'll save Caril if I can pray for her tonight," said Mrs. Pansy

Street, grandmother of Caril Fugate, 14-year-old student charged with first degree murder.

"I'm superstitious that way," declared the 62-year-old widow, adding, "I couldn't pray for Barbara last Sunday night, and she turned up dead."

Mrs. Street referred to Mrs. Marion S. Bartlett, her daughter and Caril's mother, who was found shot to death Monday. Mrs. Bartlett's husband and two-year-old daughter also were found slain.

"If I can't pray for Caril, the law'll just throw away the jail house key, and that's that," she stated.

Mrs. Street, who said she works as a fry cook in a local restaurant, stated she had managed to "hold up under the strain so far."

"But when the tears begin to come," she said, "they'll flow like a river," adding, "I've had bad times before, and come through — there's nothing else to do."

Mrs. Street, who shares a one-room tenement apartment with her invalid son, said her granddaughter "just couldn't have killed her own mother and done all those other things."

"All she wanted was just go to school and be a nurse — and Granny was ready to help her make it.

"But now," she said, "that money'll go into coffins for Marion, Barbara and Betty Jean," adding, "The baby'll be buried with her mother."

"I can't help but think Caril was forced to go with this boy, and that he was going to kill her too," Mrs. Street said of Charles Starkweather, Caril's 19-year-old companion.

"We didn't want her to go with that fellow after they had a few spats, even though he looked like a nice enough boy."

— Star, Jan. 30, 1958

Journal reporter Marj Marlette checked with friends and schoolmates and found little really defining information about the girl:

From Junior High to Jail In Week — Caril's Tragedy

Early last week Caril Fugate was an eighth grader at Whittier Junior High — an eighth grader with a ribbon in her hair and an attendance record better than any she'd had in the past several years.

Soon the same small, brown-haired teenager will be under detention in Lincoln — an unknown quantity in the shocking murders committed by her longtime boyfriend, Charles Starkweather.

No one can say exactly what Caril Fugate is like.

Her friends are loyal. And of youngsters who were merely acquainted with her, some consider her "quite nice" while others "didn't like her."

At 14 and a half, she is described as having a "certain elfish

Caril Fugate (left) and sister Barbara Von Busch with their father, William Fugate, and their stepmother, Dorothy.

charm" and the problems of popularity of all half-grown people.

She also, it is felt, had had some unhappy experiences and had come from an unfortunate background in which divorce and financial problems were evident.

Her mother — one of the first persons killed in the murder spree — divorced her father in 1951, when Caril was not quite eight.

He is still living in Lincoln.

Subsequently, her mother got county assistance for herself and her two daughters, and later remarried. (Caril has one older sister besides the little half-sister who was killed along with her mother and stepfather.)

The family apparently moved around a lot, since she attended school at Bancroft, Elliot, Park, Hayward and Belmont as well as Whittier.

At school, she was somewhat slow. But, it is reported, she "worked awfully hard" trying to bring her work up to par.

She appeared to be anxious to cooperate in any efforts to help her.

Though not legally old enough to drive one, Caril liked cars, and Starkweather let her drive his folks'. Because they objected to this, he left home after an argument.

A week ago Tuesday was Caril's last day of school. On that day, Starkweather says, he killed her mother, stepfather, and little sister. After that, she says, he held her captive until — and through — the terrorizing spree in which he killed seven more people "in self-defense" because he got mad at them.

Caril's innocence or involvement in any of the tragedies is yet to be determined. (A murder charge is still on file against her in Lancaster County Court.)

— *Journal, Jan. 31, 1958*

That same reporter, who may have gotten to know Caril better than any other media person, was to say many years later that Caril was "no innocent."

An uncle, who took in a puppy found inside the Marion Bartlett home after the murders, told a reporter:

Caril 'Not Cruel' — Kin; Loves Animals, Tots, Uncle Says

"She isn't a cruel-minded person. She loves children and animals."

This was Caril Ann Fugate's uncle, Frank Street, speaking as he described what happened to the little collie puppy that police found inside the Marion Bartlett home at 924 Belmont — the same address at which the bodies of Caril Ann's mother, stepfather and little sister were found in outbuildings on the evening of Jan. 27.

Frank Street said his family have the puppy at their home at 720 Nance, and that the wistful-looking dog is Caril Ann's.

"Caril Ann has always loved animals, just as she has always loved children," Street said.

"She bought the puppy, which she named King, with money she made from baby-sitting," the girl's uncle explained. He said he understood it was a pedigreed dog and cost Caril Ann $25.

"Caril has been baby-sitting for three or four years," he said, adding that his niece often used some of this earned money to buy gifts for the two-year-old sister, Betty Jean Bartlett, one of the first murder victims discovered.

He recalled how she was "like a big mother" to many little children.

"They loved her, too," he said, and added this was how his own 10-year-old son and 8-, 6- and 2-year-old daughters felt, too, about their cousin, Caril Ann.

The uncle said his family would keep King until things were straightened out.

"If Caril Ann gets out of this mess and wants King back, she can have him," Street said, "or her sister, Barbara (Mrs. Robert Von Busch), may want him later. Anyway, there is no need for Caril to worry. We will see that King has a home with us as long as he needs it."

— Journal, Feb. 6, 1958

Caril Fugate's father, a school custodian, told a Star reporter during Starkweather's trial:

Father Says Caril Fugate Feared Guns

Could 14-year-old Caril Ann Fugate wield and operate a gun to any degree of efficiency? Her father, William Fugate, says, "No."

Mr. Fugate, Lincoln schools custodian, told The Star Thursday, "I think Caril is even afraid of guns. She never had a rifle or a gun of any kind, and she never fired one until last winter when she went hunting with Charles and some friends."

Accused killer Charles Starkweather had stated in pre-trial testimony that Caril held a gun while in the car driven by Robert Jensen, 17, and Carol King, 16, of Bennet, who were both found slain.

Charles had further stated that Caril held a .410 shotgun while driving away from the murder scene.

"Caril only shot a rifle two or three times when she went hunting last winter," her father said. "Why, she even hurt her finger once on a B-B gun and had to have it fixed at the hospital. I can prove this."

When asked whether he thought Caril had persuaded Charles not to give himself up, he said that he didn't know. "I wouldn't want to say or do anything that might hurt Caril in any way. She's my daughter," he said.

— Star, May 9, 1958

Less than two weeks after his daughter's arrest, Caril Fugate's father took school books to her at the Lincoln State Hospital so that she could keep up on her eighth-grade school work while awaiting her preliminary hearing. His wife, Caril's stepmother, took the girl a two-pound box of candy.

It was Caril Fugate's grandmother, Mrs. Pansy Street, and her uncle, Frank Street, who asked the Lancaster County Court to be named guardians of the 14-year-old girl accused of murder.

From these skimpy details, Lincoln newspaper readers began to evaluate Caril Fugate, the 14-year-old who had fled Charles Starkweather's car after a three-day shooting spree, running to a deputy sheriff's car in Wyoming and shouting, "Save me, save me. He's going to shoot me, too."

She also told the deputy then that Starkweather "held me hostage" and that "I was afraid he was going to take me to Washington and kill me."

The deputy quoted the girl as saying she'd "seen" all nine Nebraska killings, that she'd not been allowed out of the car since she and Starkweather left Nebraska, and that she was hungry, thirsty and tired.

"She didn't appear to be hurt physically. Her face and hands showed no indications that she had been hit or harmed in any way," the officer said. "I don't know how much to believe really, but I have the feeling she was telling the truth as we tried to catch up with Starkweather."

But other opinions were expressed early on. Lincoln Police Chief Joe Carroll said Caril Fugate had ample opportunity to get away from Starkweather several times during the eight days they were together.

Immediately after Starkweather was taken to the Wyoming jail, the suspected killer told officers, "The girl had no part in it. Don't get rough with her." But only a day later, while being returned to Lincoln, he was telling police he "didn't hold a gun on her or tell her what to say" and "she could have got away but didn't try."

On that return trip to Lincoln, Caril Fugate, riding in a separate car, "seemed to get angrier all the time at Chuck," a policeman said.

And before Starkweather had gotten back to Lincoln, he had reversed himself and said the girl was a willing companion on the murder spree, according to Lancaster County Sheriff Merle Karnopp. Later, Starkweather added that at various times Caril had held a gun on victims, and in one later "confession" he claimed she was the one who had killed Carol King of Bennet and the shoe salesman who was slain in Wyoming.

Caril Fugate continued to maintain her innocence, saying she had not known her family had been killed, that when she turned away visitors at the door of her home she did so as Starkweather held her at gunpoint.

It took a jury trial to settle the question of whether Caril Fugate was a willing accomplice or another victim. The jury decided she was guilty, although it recommended a life sentence rather than death for the then 15-year-old girl.

Starkweather (foreground) reads a book on psychiatry as his defense attorneys question Dr. Edwin Coats (rear) about his sanity.

Teen-agers on trial

TWO-WEEK TRIAL, DEATH SENTENCE

On March 10, 1958, District Judge Harry A. Spencer appointed two Lincoln attorneys, T. Clement Gaughan and William F. Matschullat, to represent Charles Starkweather in his trial for the murder of Bennet teen-ager Robert Jensen. They were to serve Starkweather until he dismissed them exactly one year later as he awaited a hearing before the Nebraska Board of Pardons. Gaughan and Matschullat told the court they thought they would be ready for the trial to begin as scheduled in May. Even before their appointment, the county attorney announced that his list of prospective witnesses against Starkweather probably would exceed 40 people.

The legal proceedings against Charles Starkweather began March 26. Del Snodgrass of the Journal reported the five-minute event this way:

Starkweather Plea — I'm Innocent

Charles R. Starkweather pleaded innocent in Lancaster County District Court Wednesday to two first degree murder counts.

The redheaded 19-year-old youth was arraigned before District Judge Harry Spencer.

Approximately 50 spectators were on hand in the courtroom to witness the proceedings, but many seats were vacant.

The actual arraignment took only five minutes. Starkweather was ushered into Sheriff Merle Karnopp's office where newsmen were allowed to take photogaphs.

Starkweather, who has confessed to the slayings of 11 persons, obligingly smiled for the photograghers, puffed on a cigarette and said a few words to his two court-appointed attorneys.

Starkweather, his hair grown much longer since his first haircut

Meeting before Starkweather's trial were (from left, seated) Chief Deputy Lancaster County Attorney Dale Fahrenbruch; Dr. Robert Stein, psychiatrist; County Attorney Elmer Scheele; (standing) Dr. Edwin Coats, psychiatrist; and Charles Munson, psychologist.

On the defense side were (from left) Dr. Nathan Greenbaum, psychiatrist; Dr. John F. Steinman, psychiatrist; Dr. John O'Hearne, psychiatrist; and Starkweather's two court-appointed lawyers, William Matschullat and T. Clement Gaughan.

at the State Penitentiary, listened as Co. Atty. Elmer Scheele read
the court information.

The two counts are the Jan. 27 first degree murder of Robert
Jensen of Bennet, and the first degree murder of the 17-year-old
youth "while in the perpetration of a robbery."

Judge Spencer asked Starkweather if he understood the charge.
Starkweather replied, "I do."

Then, when Spencer asked the youth how he wished to plead,
Atty. T. Clement Gaughan said Starkweather wished to plead innocent to both counts.

Gaughan added that the defense "reserves any further pleas as
to the not guilty part of it to any time before the start of the trial."

It was believed that remark might indicate the defense will later
enter a plea of innocent by reason of insanity.

Spencer ordered Starkweather held for trial at the jury term
tentatively set for May 5.

Both Starkweather's court-appointed attorneys, Gaughan and
William F. Matschullat, said they are still looking for one or more
psychiatrists to represent the defense at Starkweather's trial.

Two Omaha psychiatrists and an Omaha psychologist recently
declined appointments by Judge Spencer.

— *Journal, March 26, 1958*

There was difficulty obtaining psychiatric specialists to examine the defendant. Three of the first four named withdrew because they would have had to
act for either the defense or the prosecution and could not appear as "friends
of the court." Eventually, a Lincoln psychiatrist, Dr. John Steinman, and two
Kansas City men, a psychologist and a psychiatrist, did the examinations, completed in mid-April.

Prior to the trial, there were stories about a statement by Lancaster County
Attorney Elmer Scheele that he had made no promises to Starkweather for his
testimony, and about the fact that no photographs could be taken in the courtroom. Artist Sally Raglin provided courtroom sketches to the Journal throughout both Starkweather's and Fugate's trials.

On Saturday, May 3, with the trial due to begin the following Monday, defense attorneys announced that Starkweather would take the stand in his own
behalf. Defense attorneys also disclosed a note written by Starkweather on a
wall in the Scotts Bluff County Jail, where he had been kept overnight on his
way back to Lincoln after his capture. High points of the cryptic note: "Charles
kill 9, all men. Caril Kill 2, all girls."

The trial began quietly, as The Star reported Tuesday morning:

Starkweather Attitude: Interested Bystander

Charles Starkweather went on trial for his life Monday with the
attitude of an interested bystander.

Dressed casually in a light tan suit, white shirt and figured tie,

Starkweather started his first day in court unsmiling, head lowered, but cheered up after preliminaries of choosing a panel of jurors proceeded.

Seated with him, and more attentive to his moves than to court proceedings, was his mother, Helen Starkweather, who like her son looked pale against the tanned faces of surrounding law officers and attorneys.

The key figure in the court drew the attention of most of the prospective jurors who, when called to take seats in the front of the courtroom for questioning, almost immediately glanced at the red-headed youth or stared at him fixedly.

Again and again County Attorney Elmer Scheele put the question to the jurors, "Would you, if you believed this man guilty, be willing to impose a death penalty?" Charles Starkweather seemed either to ignore the meaning of this query or to be oblivious to Scheele's questioning.

Mrs. Starkweather explained that her husband's absence Monday was due to his work, and she expressed concern at leaving the rest of her family for the long trial period.

She smiled happily at the attorneys who pointed out that "now you can be close to Charles all day" and said she thought he looked fine, "although he hates that suit."

As the questioning and "challenge for cause" dismissals narrowed down the crowd, the remaining men and women showed by their facial expressions that they were mentally answering the questions themselves.

Only two of the prospective jurors questioned said they had not formed a prior opinion on the case, but a majority of the remaining ones admitted they could put aside their opinions to judge the case on the court evidence.

— *Star, May 6, 1958*

Shortly before jury selection began, the defense attorneys changed Starkweather's plea from innocent to innocent by reason of insanity, despite reluctance voiced by the defendant and by members of his family.

Jury selection took all of the first three days of the trial, but there was one particularly dramatic development, reported in The Star:

'Caril Wouldn't Give Up,' Starkweather Statement Claims

Killer Charles Starkweather was quoted Tuesday afternoon by his defense attorneys as saying he wanted to give himself up after the fifth and sixth slayings of his January murder rampage but that he was talked out of it by his girlfriend.

Attorneys T. Clement Gaughan and William F. Matschullat said the statement was contained in a signed statement which Starkweather gave county authorities following his arrest. Stark-

Starkweather wore a suit — but not his customary cowboy boots — for trial.

weather was quoted as saying 14-year-old Caril Fugate tried to talk him out of giving up and that he finally agreed with her.

Starkweather hints in the statement that he changed his mind because Caril had a .410 shotgun on her lap, although he said she did not point it at him.

Starkweather's father, Guy Starkweather of 3025 N, told The Star several weeks ago that his 19-year-old son had wanted to give himself up after the deaths of Robert Jensen, 17, and Carol King, 16, both of Bennet, but that Caril Fugate disagreed and Charles was afraid to press the point because she also had a gun.

But until Tuesday's after-court disclosure the persons connected with the case had refused to comment on the story.

In another part of the statement released by the court-appointed defense attorneys, Starkweather is quoted as saying that Caril Fugate had helped guard Jensen and Miss King while in the Jensen car en route to the school cellar where the two Bennet students later were fatally shot.

The talk of giving up, Gaughan said, came after Jensen and Miss King had been killed and Starkweather and Caril were driving back towards Lincoln on State 2. They were arguing, according to the statement, but Gaughan declined to say why.

— Star, May 7, 1958

On Wednesday, with the jury still not picked, Starkweather answered a newsman's questions, throwing further confusion on what he would claim in his trial. The Star's story:

'Never Killed Half Those People' — Starkweather

Accused slayer Charles Starkweather told a Lincoln newsman, "I never killed half of those people they are talking about up there."

The 19-year-old former garbage-hauler, linked with 11 murders, told part-time International News Service correspondent Don Wright "those people at the courthouse are confused up there."

Starkweather answered three questions for Wright before officers terminated the interview at the Lincoln Police Station where the red-haired youth receives his noon meal during his murder trial.

It was one of the few occasions in Starkweather's life when he bothered to reply to a reporter's question.

— Star, May 8, 1958

The pace of the Starkweather murder trial picked up the following afternoon as the prosecutor, Lancaster County Attorney Elmer Scheele, and defense attorney T. Clement Gaughan made their opening statements before the jury of eight women and four men.

Twelve members of the Starkweather jury listen to testimony.

Starkweather Was Suffering From 'Delusion' — Defense

Charles Starkweather was suffering from a "delusion" and therefore was "legally insane" when he fatally shot 17-year-old Robert Jensen of Bennet Jan. 27 in a storm cellar east of Bennet, defense attorney T. Clement Gaughan claimed Thursday afternoon.

Gaughan, in his opening statement for the defense before the jury of eight women and four men chosen to hear the first degree murder trial in Lancaster County Court, did not specify what type of delusion the 19-year-old redhead is supposed to be suffering. But he said important things to the average person are "little things" to Starkweather while unimportant things are "big" to him.

Gaughan said that Starkweather, for example, was quite concerned as to what type of shoes he could wear at his murder trial (he reportedly wanted to wear his cowboy boots but was not allowed to), but that the former garbage collector was little concerned with being on trial for his life.

Gaughan said the defense would not deny that Starkweather killed Jensen. "This is not a 'who' murder case," Gaughan said, "but a 'why' murder case."

Gaughan also declared again that Starkweather himself will be called to the stand to testify in his own defense. Several other members of his family are also expected to testify for the defense.

He painted a picture of Starkweather as an underprivileged boy

— who wore hand-me-down clothes, never had a bicycle or spending money — who is sub-normal mentally and possibly could have a brain tumor or "pressure on the brain."

Gaughan said Starkweather was struck in the head several years ago by a piece of metal which had broken off a baling machine. Since then, the attorney said, the youth has often had "serious headaches."

But Starkweather, who opposes basing his defense on insanity, has refused to undergo medical tests to see if he does have a brain tumor or brain injury, Gaughan said. But it has been learned that he does have a "perforated ear drum," he added.

Starkweather, Gaughan declared, claims that he shot the unarmed Jensen in "self defense." Never at any time did Starkweather intend to kill him, Gaughan said Starkweather claims, but when Jensen came "flying up" the cellar stairs at Starkweather, he shot him in "self defense."

This account, however, differed sharply with the account Co. Atty. Elmer Scheele gave of the murder, which Starkweather is charged with, in his opening statement.

Scheele admitted that Starkweather in a written statement claimed that he shot Jensen when Jensen "came at him" after being ordered down into the cellar with his girlfriend, Carol King, 16, also of Bennet. The two youths reportedly had offered the hitchhiking Starkweather and Caril Fugate a ride into Bennet, and were robbed and then forced into at gunpoint to drive to the storm cellar.

Scheele said he will introduce evidence to prove that Jensen was "shot from behind six times" with a .22 caliber pump rifle held by Starkweather. All the bullets, Scheele said, lodged in Jensen's body in a space about 1¼ inches in diameter.

Just as Starkweather must be considered innocent until proven otherwise, Scheele said, so must he be considered sane until some evidence to the contrary is introduced. Scheele assured the eight women and four men jurors that the state will have "competent evidence to show Starkweather knew the difference between the nature and quality of his act" in shooting Jensen.

The legal test of insanity, in brief, is whether or not the accused knew the nature and quality of his act and knew right from wrong when the alleged crime was committed.

— *Star, May 9, 1958*

The Star also carried Starkweather's reaction to the opening statements:

Starkweather Angers, But Maintains Silence

Charles Starkweather seemed to realize for the first time Thursday that he was on trial for his life.

The pint-sized defendant showed all the signs of violent anger but maintained silence by biting his lip as his attorney, T. Clement Gaughan, outlined his defense as insanity — "delusions" he evidently has been suffering for the past few years.

As Gaughan quietly outlined the defense case to the jurors using the words "diseased and defective mind," "maladjusted" and "abnormal," the 19-year-old's face grew red, he grasped the edge of the counsel table, staring fixedly and with apparent hatred at Gaughan.

During Gaughan's brief opening statement, the youth remained restive and obviously unhappy. He was without the half-smirk, half-smile which had become his trademark during the trial previously.

As the defendant marched out of the courtroom at the end of Thursday's sessions, his prison pallor was still replaced by an angry flush which clashed with his flame-colored hair.

His mother, smiling nervously but seemingly unshaken by the opening trial statements, stood apart and watched her son being led out in handcuffs, surrounded by guards.

She had glanced at Starkweather only two or three times during the afternoon when Gaughan had referred to an IQ test which placed her son's intelligence at "only a point or two above an idiot" and when Gaughan had told jurors that her son would take the stand in his own defense.

— *Star, May 9, 1958*

Starkweather's mother maintained her own control only with difficulty:

'Charles Only Showed When He Was Mad'

Helen Starkweather sat sadly in court Tuesday, keeping control with an effort as Co. Atty. Elmer Scheele read the statement in which her son, Charles, detailed his criminal career.

Though she had shown concern with Defense Attorney T. Clement Gaughan's contention that Charles is "insane," she said she would rather not comment on the insanity plea.

About Charles' lack of remorse for the murders, though, she did assert:

"A person doesn't have to show their emotions to feel them. And Charlie was always like that. He only showed when he was mad."

She will testify for the defense in a day or two. Some friends of Charles will not be called though, she said, because — she said Charles told her — the defense attorney said the boys' and girls' "IQs were no higher than his."

Gaughan has claimed that Charles' IQ is only a point or two above an idiot.

— *Journal, May 13, 1958*

The first testimony in the case came late Thursday, and the trial moved ahead swiftly, with The Star reporting in its Saturday editions that by Friday afternoon Scheele had called half of his listed 28 witnesses. Prosecution testimony was finished the following Tuesday morning.

During the noon recess on Friday, Starkweather smashed a camera into a photographer's face. He later apologized but was heard to mutter, "Next time I'll kick you in the head."

Introduced into evidence the following Monday was a letter that Starkweather purportedly wrote in the Ward home and addressed to his parents. The defendant was reported as writing that Caril " 'helped me a lot' but didn't do any of the actual killings."

Testimony was heard from victim Robert Jensen's father; from a pathologist who reported six bullets entered the youth's head near the ear, three of them behind the ear; from ballistics experts; from the person who found Jensen's body, and from witnesses to statements by the defendant.

Defense testimony began on Wednesday, and defense attorneys began to build their case that Starkweather suffered from delusions and was legally insane. Part of their case was based on the conflicting "confessions" written by the defendant; by Friday of that week seven such documents, totaling 347 pages, had been introduced.

One such statement:

'For Law Only' Letter Tells Of First Slayings

Here is the unedited text of the letter which Wyoming officials found on Charles Starkweather when he was captured. It was addressed "for the law only."

This is for the cops or lawmen who fines us. Caril and I are writting this so that you and everybody will know what has happen. On Tues day 7 days befor you have see the bodies of my mom, dad, and baby sister. There dead because of me and Chuck.

Chuck came down that day happy and full of jokes but when he came in mom said for him to get out and never come back.

Chuck look at her and said why. At that my dad got mad and begin to hit him and was pushing him all over the room. Then Chuck got mad and there was no stopping him. He had his gun with him cause him and my dad was going hunting.

Well Chuck pull it and (picture of bullet shown here) come out and my dad drop to the floor. At this my mom was so mad that she had a (picture of knife) and was going to cut him.

She knot the gun from Chuck's hands. Chuck just stood there saying he was sorry he didn't want to do it. I got Chuck's gun and stop my mom from killing Chuck. Betty Jean was yelling so loud I hit her with the gun about 10 times. She would not stop. Chuck had the (picture of a knife) so he was about 10 steps from her. He let it go. It stopped somewhere by her head.

Me and Chuck just look at them for about 4 hours. Then we

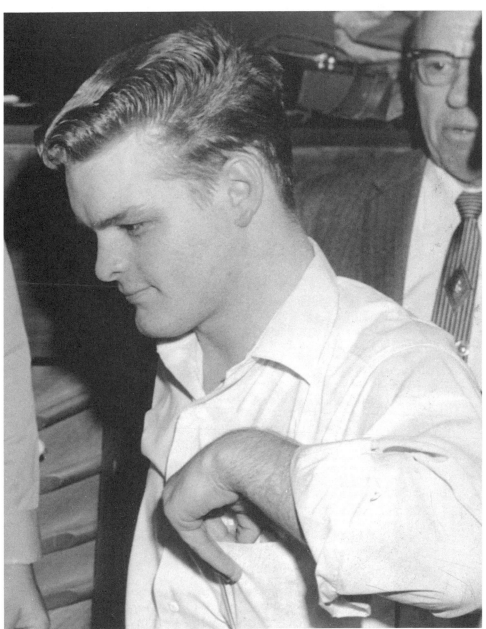

Starkweather leaves courtroom during afternoon recess on May 15, 1958.

wrapped them and pulled them out in the house in back. My sisters and everone eles we not believe this but its true and I say it by God.

Then me and Chuck live with each other and Monday the day the bodies were found, we were going to kill ourselves. But Bob Von Bruck and everybody would not say away. And hate my older sister and Bob for what they are. They all ways wanted me to stop going with Chuck show that some kid Bob Kwen could go with me. Chuck and I are sorry for what we did but know we're going to the end.

I feel sorry for Bar to have a ask like Bob.

I and Caril are sorry for what happen, cause I have hurt everybody cause of it and so has Caril. But I am saying one thing. Everybody that came out there was luckie there not dead even Caril's sister.

Chuck S. and Caril F.

So far we have killed 7 persons.

— Star, May 13, 1958

Also introduced by the defense was part of what the Journal called the "Wyoming confession," detailing the events in the Ward household:

Ward Deaths Detailed In Wyoming Confession

The part of Charles Starkweather's "Wyoming confession" — introduced by the defense Wednesday — relating to the Ward murders includes the following (copied verbatim from the original):

". . . that night we stay in the car it was cold but we nake i said we was going to have to stay somewhere that day cause of the car we had

"we drove all over thinking what house would be the best place to stay show about 8:30 in the morning & pick out the one on 24th there was two person there they about had a drop dead when i said we was going to spend the day there.

"they said they would be nice and nothing would happen like calling the cops. thy were unith about 2:00 that after noon the one lady was up stairs and was there about 20 nin i went on up to see her she niss me about ½" with a .22 cal. gun she just look at ne and back up and began to run all i had was that kilfe so it go at her it stop right in her back.

"The naid was there i tie tie her up and left her lay-ing on the beb the dog was there to i had to hit him to keep him from barking.

"the naid was there i tie her up all but the feet and told caril to nake her lie down on the bed and tie her to the beb.

"About 6:30 or 7:00 that night the nan cane hone i told hin not to nove but he did any way we was by the basement steps we got into a fight he got he gun from ne show i push hin doun the basenent steps.

"the gun landed on the foor and went off he got and start for it but i was frist he pick out iron and i said if i had to c'll kill hin show he lay it doun i said for hin to walk back up the stairs we was to tie hin up and leave toun.

"he start to walk up the stairs he got ½ way amd begin to run i shot hin in the back one's the he stop i told hin the next tine would be it he got to the top of the stairs and ran for the front door he had it ½ way open when i shot hin.

"he was laying there naking funny noise i told caril to get a banket and cover hin up.

"we got some food from there and left — last night was heading for Washington, state we got as far as here when we heard about the fine the bodys of the 3 persons, but when i lelf ther was only 1 dead person in that house.

— Journal, May 14, 1958

In another, a letter from Starkweather in prison to Scheele, the defendant reportedly charged that Caril Fugate had shot the King girl, that his girlfriend "was the most trigger-happy person I ever seen," and said, "I'll be convicted for what I did and that's OK . . . . But I'll be damned if I'll be sentenced for what I didn't do."

Starkweather himself took the stand May 15:

Killings Were Self Defense

Accused mass killer Charles Starkweather took the witness stand Thursday at his first degree murder trial, and claimed "I killed them all in self defense, the ones I killed."

Asked by his defense attorney if he was sorry for any of the killings he refused to answer. But the 19-year-old redhead said in answer to another question that if his victims had not done something to "threaten" him they would all still be alive today.

— Star, May 16, 1958

Psychiatrists and a psychologist took the stand for the defense on Monday of the second week of the trial.

Psychologist Says 'People Have No Meaning to Starkweather'

"People do not mean anything to Charles Starkweather," a Kansas City psychologist testified at the confessed slayer's trial Monday.

A person "means no more to him than a stick," declared Dr. Nathan Greenbaum, the only defense witness on the stand during the morning session.

Starkweather, Greenbaum testified, is suffering from a "severe mental illness" and did not know the difference between right and wrong during the January murder spree.

The Kansas Citian said he tested Starkweather twice — for 8½ hours Apr. 9 and for about 2 hours Sunday night.

He said the tests made him arrive at the following conclusions:

1. Starkweather is devoid of many of the basic feelings necessary for harmonious living with others.

The youth, he said, "has grown up in a vacuum . . . apart and isolated from society."

2. Starkweather "lacks the capacity for control" which makes the normal individual "stop and think about the consequences" of what he does.

"Had a person such as Starkweather been brought to my office before any crime was committed," Dr. Greenbaum declared, "I would have said the person was capable of serious criminal acts and should have been put away under maximum security."

3. Starkweather is "unable to premeditate, he jumps from impulse to the act," Greenbaum testified.

The psychologist said the red-haired youth on trial for his life is incapable of experiencing any feelings of remorse for the persons he has admitted murdering.

On cross examination by Co. Atty. Elmer Scheele, Greenbaum said he could not give a name to Starkweather's "mental illness."

"I could call it something, perhaps the XYZ disease," the psychologist said, "but that would make it (the disease) suddenly appear."

Greenbaum did testify, however, that he believes Starkweather had the ability to think about ways of evading apprehension during the murder spree.

On direct examination, Greenbaum likened Starkweather to a "a wild beast brought out of the jungle who has assumed a 'crust' of domestication."

Starkweather slumped down in his chair and rarely looked at Greenbaum while the psychologist was testifying.

Dr. John O'Hearne, Kansas City psychiatrist, testified Monday afternoon that Starkweather was incapable of having any premeditation before murdering Robert W. Jensen, Jan. 27th.

He said he believed Starkweather became "a wild animal" after the first in the series of January murders.

O'Hearne testified that he had asked Charlie how he felt this morning.

Charlie replied, he said, that "I don't like it."

He also quoted Charlie as saying, "If I had a grenade (bomb) . . . I could kill Greenbaum."

When O'Hearne asked him about the other people, he said Charlie replied, "To hell with them."

O'Hearne also said that Charlie also wanted to shoot his former employer and his attorneys.

Dr. O'Hearne testified that Starkweather "is very much afraid of a man, particularly a big man."

At the moment of Jensen's death, he continued, Starkweather was not capable of knowing the enormity of the act.

He added that Starkweather "is more concerned about being declared insane than going to the electric chair."

The psychiatrist added that "pumping bullets into a human is no different to Starkweather than pumping bullets into a rabbit."

— Journal, May 19, 1958

The Journal reported the testimony of another psychiatrist, Dr. John Steinman, as follows:

Steinman testified he believes Starkweather sincerely believes he killed all his victims in self-defense.

"Does the fact that Robert W. Jensen was shot in the right side of the head indicate the self-defense argument is imaginary and a further indication of the defendant's diseased mind?" Matschullat asked.

"I believe it does," Steinman replied.

The psychiatrist also testified Starkweather shows indications of being paranoid.

"An individual should not turn his back on a person suffering from paranoia," he said.

"A paranoid is distrustful of a person in retreat and feels the individual may return to harm him."

Starkweather, Steinman continued, shows much ability in some fields, noting that Dr. Greenbaum testified Monday that one test given Starkweather showed the youth's IQ 97.

But the misspellings and grammatical errors in his notes and letters, Steinman said, "indicate the status of his mind when he is under great stress."

Matschullat asked Steinman if he believes Starkweather was capable of premeditation at the moment he killed Jensen.

"I do not believe he was," the psychiatrist answered.

He added that during times of stress Starkweather "is like a child of 5 with a popgun saying, 'Bang, you're dead.'"

Co. Atty. Elmer Scheele, during cross examination in an attempt to prove Starkweather was capable of intent and premeditation, asked Steinman if Starkweather planned to take Jensen's car.

"Yes," the psychiatrist answered.

"Did he (Starkweather) carry out that intention?" Scheele asked.

"Yes, I believe he did," Steinman replied.

Scheele also gained the admission from the psychiatrist that Starkweather was planning to murder Marion Bartlett, the stepfather of Caril Fugate and one of the first four murder victims, when the youth went to a phone and called Bartlett's employer to say the man would not be at work for a few days.

"Isn't it true that every murderer justifies his acts in his own mind?" Scheele asked.

"Yes," Steinman replied, "but it would seem Starkweather would think of a more reasonable alibi than self-defense" in the death of the Bartlett's 2-year-old daughter.

— *Journal, May 20, 1958*

County Attorney Scheele countered with other psychiatric testimony, most notably by Lincoln psychiatrist Robert Stein, just before the trial recessed on Wednesday:

Dr. Stein, the state's star witness called to testify Starkweather is sane, pronounced the youth "legally sane" on Jan. 27 when Robert W. Jensen of Bennet was murdered in a storm cellar.

Dr. Stein testified that Starkweather has a "personality disorder" but that he is "not a fit person for confining to a mental hospital."

Starkweather seemed unconcerned about the psychiatrist's testimony. He looked through the psychiatry textbook at the counsel table and occasionally leaned forward to whisper with Dr. John Steinman.

A defense witness, Dr. Steinman said Starkweather was asking him questions about psychiatric terms.

Dr. Stein testified during questioning by Co. Atty. Elmer Scheele that Starkweather "knew the difference between right and wrong and the nature and quality of his acts."

"Is murder a normal act?" Scheele asked.

"No," Stein replied.

"But is it (murder) in itself a criterion of insanity?" the attorney questioned.

A clinical psychologist testified Tuesday afternoon that Starkweather was "legally sane" on Jan. 27 when Robert W. Jensen of Bennet was murdered.

He was Charles Munson of the Lincoln State Hospital staff, the first prosecution witness called to the stand after the defense for Charles Starkweather rested its case.

Munson testified he interviewed Starkweather on two occasions — Apr. 2 and Apr. 10 — at the Nebraska Penitentiary.

Dr. Edwin Coats testified he does not believe Starkweather is suffering from any "delusions or hallucinations."

He described Starkweather as a "cooperative, pleasant young man who readily admits the crimes with which he is charged."

"Did Starkweather understand the enormity of his situation?"

Starkweather's mother, Helen, testified in his defense.

Scheele asked.

"I believe he did know and knew the consequences for the acts he committed," Dr. Coats replied.

Dr. Coats also testified he does not believe Starkweather has a "diseased or defective mind."

"But another person in your profession might disagree," Gaughan said on cross-examination.

"That's right," Dr. Coats said.

— Journal, May 21, 1958

Closing arguments came on Thursday. Portions of the Journal's report:

Jury Ponders Verdict After Death Penalty Is Demanded

Lancaster County Attorney Elmer Scheele late Thursday asked for the death sentence in the Charles Starkweather murder trial.

"Can we take a chance and gamble with the safety of persons in this community?" Scheele asked the jury.

He said the death sentence is the "only safe solution, the one answer, for the fate of the confessed slayer."

Scheele's closing argument followed an emotional plea made by Defense Attorney T. Clement Gaughan for Starkweather's life.

Scheele told the jury that "I could take you" to the scenes of the December and January murders in the Lincoln area and "show you some gruesome sights I never expected to see."

He pleaded with (the) jury, "Don't be misled by an age-old trick and sacrifice the interests of society by returning an innocent by reason of insanity verdict."

The defense, Scheele continued, "has skipped all around the world in an attempt to take your minds away from the evidence in the case."

"Can't you see what a hoax it is to persuade you into grabbing at the straw of insanity?" he asked the jury.

Scheele declared that evidence by both defense and prosecution psychiatrists and psychologists shows that Starkweather was legally sane and was capable of premeditation when he killed Robert W. Jensen.

He said the alleged "short circuit" in Starkweather's mind is "pure sham and another deliberate attempt to pull the wool over your eyes."

Defense Attorney Gaughan broke into tears Thursday afternoon as he compared his own life with that of Charles Starkweather's.

"I grew up to be exactly like Charles Starkweather," Gaughan declared. "I hated everybody and everything and I could lick anybody — that society treated me as it treated Charles Starkweather.

"But the good Lord gave me, possibly, a little better parents," he said.

Gaughan, in his closing argument, took only 50 minutes to plead for the life of the confessed slayer.

"The Bible commandment which says 'Thou shalt not kill,'" Gaughan told the jury, "applies just as much to you as to Starkweather."

The attorney also told the jury that if they returned the death sentence he would arrange to have them "at the death house at the Nebraska Penitentiary for the electrocution."

Gaughan gave a vivid account of the youth sitting in the chair, "his head shaved, and his hair standing on end as the electricity goes through his body."

Gaughan also told the jury, "If you feel you want the life of this boy, Caril Fugate deserves the same punishment."

Defense Atty. William F. Matschullat made an impassioned plea against capital punishment Thursday during closing arguments.

Matschullat pictured Starkweather as a person with a "sick, ill feeble mind."

"Are we going to push this boy down in the electric chair if he has a deranged mind?" Matschullat asked. "Why should we kill the boy? Let's kill the devil in him!"

— Journal, May 22, 1958

The jury was given five choices:
- Guilty of first-degree murder (killing with premeditation and malice).
- Guilty of second-degree murder (killing without premeditation but with malice).
- Guilty of manslaughter (killing with neither premeditation nor malice).
- Innocent by reason of insanity (killing while not knowing the difference between right and wrong).
- Innocent.

The jury received the case at 5:24 p.m. Thursday, May 22, and retired for the night at 10:07 without reaching a verdict. Jurors reconvened Friday morning and came in with the verdict at 2:14 p.m. They said they had been agreed on guilt from the beginning but had divided on the question of punishment, taking four 11-1 votes before reaching a verdict for death on the fifth ballot.

The Star's headline:

MASS-KILLER STARKWEATHER TO PAY WITH LIFE

The Star's story reported that as the Starkweather family left the Courthouse, Guy Starkweather told his wife, Helen, and son Rodney, "We ought to go someplace and eat a big, fat steak."

DEATH POSTPONED, BUT ONLY BRIEFLY

On June 7, 1958, Charles Starkweather was sentenced to die in Nebraska's electric chair on Dec. 17. He would be the 20th person executed under the state's capital punishment laws, the first in six years, and the 12th to die in the chair. There were predictions that his appeals would take about a year, the predictions based on the fact that in the most recent death penalty case the appeals process had postponed that execution about a year.

The judge noted that he was setting Starkweather's execution date later than would be usual because the Nebraska Supreme Court would be in recess during July and August. Under a new state law, the death penalty case would be appealed automatically to the Supreme Court.

Defense attorneys announced that the appeal would not be carried beyond the Supreme Court "unless somebody comes up with some funds," noting that the state of Nebraska would not pay for appeals beyond its high court. In northwest Nebraska's Sandhills a group announced, perhaps with tongue in cheek, that it would raise money for Starkweather's defense; a largely Lincoln group previously had obtained a new trial for another man, Loyd Grandsinger, convicted of murder in the Sandhills area.

Mrs. Starkweather wrote a letter to the editor of The Star, saying her son blamed his attorneys for his death sentence and claiming that, in the first 42 days after they were appointed, the defense attorneys had visited him only six times.

On July 5, the defense attorneys filed an appeal with the state Supreme Court, claiming errors during the trial. As an alternative to reversal of the conviction, they asked that the high court reduce the sentence to life, citing Starkweather's "insanity." The original execution date passed before the high court, on Dec. 19, denied the appeal and set a new execution date of March 27, 1959.

On March 2, Starkweather filed his own appeal for clemency with the state Board of Pardons and Paroles. Journal reporter Marj Marlette remembers that she furnished copies of the appeals forms to Starkweather; the newspapers noted that Starkweather made his own application, with the assistance of officials at the Penitentiary. Then, on March 10, Starkweather fired his attorneys; in a letter to Lancaster District Judge Harry A. Spencer, he said he did not wish to retain "any service of" the court-appointed lawyers.

On April 21, 1959, the Pardons Board denied Starkweather's appeal for clemency and set a new execution date of May 22. The Journal's story:

Pardon Board Denies Bid For Clemency

A two-member Board of Pardons and Paroles Tuesday denied clemency to condemned killer Charles Starkweather and set his new execution date as May 22.

Upon hearing the decision, Starkweather, waiting inside the prison, said, "I half expected it."

He gave no visible sign of emotion when told of the verdict, Mrs.

Loretta Walker, administrative assistant to the board, reported.

Almost no deliberation took place as Atty. Gen. C.S. Beck and Secy. of State Frank Marsh finished making their decision minutes after Starkweather's hearing ended.

Mrs. Walker announced the refusal of clemency after the board members themselves had left the Penitentiary, where the hearing was held.

Gov. Ralph Brooks, the 3rd member and chairman of the Pardon Board, was not present during the hearing. He is in the hospital with the flu. It had not been expected that the decision would be made immediately.

Starkweather's hearing itself lasted only about an hour and a half.

White-faced and nervous, Charles told the board that he was sorry for what he had done and he would "bring them (the victims) back to life if I could."

Before the murder spree, Starkweather said, he didn't think much of life, but now "I think it's worth something."

He said he had changed in his thinking since being in prison, "Mostly by reading the Bible."

"I blame it all on my myself," he explained of his crimes.

To a question by Atty. Gen. C.S. Beck, "If you had been put in jail before, would it have made any difference?" he said, "I can't truly say — it might have."

Starkweather and his parents, who appeared for him, based much of their appeal on their feeling that he hadn't been fairly represented at his trial.

"I honestly believe if I was represented right I would have gotten life," the 20-year-old redhead told the board.

— Journal, April 21, 1959

As the new execution date approached, the Journal reported:

Starkweather Aware End Is Nearing

Twenty-year-old mass murderer Charles Starkweather will be strapped in the electric chair at 6 a.m. Friday to keep his third date with the executioner.

Two previous electrocution dates were stayed pending appeals, but any reprieve this time is not expected for the redhead convicted of the murder of a Bennet teenager.

In his death cell, Starkweather is "conscious it's getting towards the end," Acting Warden John Greenholtz says.

Though a year ago January Starkweather terrorized Lincoln, prison officials have had no trouble with the youth since his commitment. They've found him, in fact, quiet and cooperative.

The youth's last days are spent — as has been his entire year

A talented artist, Starkweather made this sketch while awaiting execution.

since a jury convicted him — in one of two death cells in the hospital section of the Penitentiary.

The other cell is empty.

His room, however, is pleasant and large (about 8x12 ft.) for a cell, with light-painted walls, a window (barred), bed, chest, table, chair and toilet facilities.

He spends his days writing, reading and drawing.

His autobiography is now hundreds of pages long. He has written some poetry, and his drawings, done free-hand, show considerable talents.

According to the chaplain, who visits him frequently, he has read his Bible daily since confinement.

Charles' parents see him often, nearly every day, and for their visits he is taken to the main building visiting room to talk to them through a screen.

Always, he is under 24-hour surveillance, and he is shaved, his hair cut, meals served, etc., only under guard.

When he goes to the chair, Charles Starkweather will be the 12th man to be electrocuted in Nebraska — the first since Roland Dean Sundahl died at 12:06 a.m. April 30, 1952, for the murder of a 16-year-old carhop.

Plans are now being completed for the execution.

The executioner, from out-of-state, has been arranged for, Acting Warden Greenholtz said. He is never identified, but it is understood he is not the same one who participated in the last two Nebraska executions.

The only witnesses to the death under state law, are six persons to be designated by the warden (in this case the acting warden) and three who may be requested by the inmate.

In addition, the warden and deputy warden are required by law to be present, they may have assistants if needed, and the executioner may also have an assistant.

Designation of the witnesses will be made in the next few days, Acting Warden Greenholtz said.

— Journal, May 17, 1959

The Starkweather autobiography referred to in that story had been partly reproduced in the March 15, 1959, issue of Parade, a magazine supplement delivered each week with the Sunday Journal and Star. Journal reporter Marj Marlette had learned that Starkweather had written an extensive account of his life, and the the Journal suggested to Parade that the magazine publish it. Parade bought the rights to the story from Guy and Helen Starkweather for $1,000, paid to them in installments to help them meet expenses.

On Thursday, May 21 — the day before the execution date — the governor announced he would not delay the execution, and U.S. District Judge Robert Van Pelt ruled that same day against an 11th-hour appeal based on Starkweather's contention that he had been denied proper legal counsel.

The Star was faced with a difficult decision. Starkweather's execution was to occur at 6 a.m. Friday, about four hours after its presses would begin to run on The Star's final edition but before most of the papers would be delivered to readers. The Star played the story straight: "Starkweather dies today; writ denied."

But the execution was not to occur just then.

Just 98 minutes before the scheduled execution — after copies of The Star had been printed — U.S. District Judge Richard Robinson of Omaha stayed the execution for two weeks to allow an appeal to the U.S. Circuit Court of Appeals. Three prominent Nebraska attorneys were appointed to represent Starkweather in the appeal. On June 4, the appeals court heard their arguments and the same day denied the appeal. The state Supreme Court set a new execution date, now 12:01 a.m. June 12.

The next delay came when a Washington attorney appealed to the U.S. Supreme Court and a justice of that court granted a one-week stay of execution.

Helen and Guy Starkweather were glad to hear news of brief reprieve.

There was speculation at that point that appeals could take another year, but a flurry of appeals ended with an execution date of 12:01 a.m. June 25, 1959, the fifth execution time set by the courts.

That time, last-minute appeals, both to the Nebraska Supreme Court and to the U.S. District Court, failed. The Star, not caught a second time with an after-deadline execution time, used this headline the morning of Thursday, June 25:

—Mass-Killer Of 11 Dies In Chair—

STARKWEATHER EXECUTED

Charles Starkweather went calmly to his death early Thursday morning in the electric chair.

The 20-year-old redhead walked briskly into the execution chamber flanked by two lawmen at 12:01 a.m.

Three minutes later, after five separate 2,200-volt electrical charges, he was pronounced dead by the attending physician, Dr. P.E. Getscher of Lincoln.

Starkweather was asked by Dep. State Penitentiary Warden John Greenholtz if he had any last words.

Starkweather shook his head and strap-like masks were placed over his eyes and mouth. Then Greenholtz signalled the out-of-state executioner to go ahead.

The youth's head was shaved and he wore a blue chambray shirt, dungarees and loafers. The left pant leg was rolled up and an electrode placed on his knee.

The only other point of electrical contact was on the headpiece.

An estimated 40 persons, including four official witnesses and about 20 newsmen, watched the state's first electrocution since Roland Dean Sundahl died Apr. 30, 1952, for the 1950 hatchet slaying of 16-year-old carhop Bonnie Lou Merril near Columbus.

Starkweather admitted pumping six bullets into Jensen's head, but his trial defense attorneys claimed he was insane and not legally responsible.

Starkweather was offered a steak for his last meal but passed it up in favor of cold cuts.

Greenholtz said Starkweather's last words when lawmen came to fetch him for his date were, "What's your hurry?"

Warden Maurice Sigler, who took over his post only Monday, called it "a normal execution, well organized."

Greenholtz said Starkweather was calm all evening and showed "no emotion whatsoever."

The Rev. Robert Klein, prison chaplain, was with Starkweather

CHARLES R. STARKWEATHER
Nov. 25, 1938 ─ June 25, 1959
Rest in peace

Charles Starkweather was buried at Wyuka Cemetery in Lincoln.

from 10:30 p.m. on, and Starkweather took part in private devotions with the minister before entering the chamber. The chaplain accompanied him on the last walk.

A police blockade at the prison entrance kept unauthorized persons from loitering in the area. About a dozen carloads of people were parked along the highway near the prison.

Greenholtz said Starkweather's body was claimed by the family and was removed immediately from the prison grounds. He said the Rev. Mr. Klein had been asked by the family to conduct funeral services for the youth.

One of Starkweather's court-appointed defense attorneys, William F. Matschullat, witnessed the execution.

Beforehand, he told newsmen he "came to pray for the accused and those close to him."

Matschullat said he believed "justice had been done." He noted nearly every possible legal device had been tried in an attempt to save the youth.

— *Star, June 25, 1959*

Private funeral services were held, and the convicted slayer was buried in Lincoln's Wyuka Cemetery.

DIFFERENT TRIAL, DIFFERENT PENALTY

Legal action against Caril Fugate began with her arraignment the Monday after she was returned to Lincoln from Wyoming. Both she and Charles Starkweather pleaded not guilty to charges of murdering Bennet teen-ager Robert Jensen.

Immediately following, there were skirmishes over the girl's legal defense. At first, she was advised by the University of Nebraska Legal Aid Bureau, run by the NU College of Law. Law College Dean Edmund O. Belsheim at one point gave Fugate advice before the court appointment of an attorney. But action the case against the 14-year-old didn't really take off until a month later when her court-appointed attorney, John McArthur, filed an action saying state law made it "mandatory" that she be tried in juvenile court, where her maximum sentence would be committal to the Girls' Training School at Geneva, Nebraska. That contention was quickly struck down by the court, and McArthur appealed, but the Nebraska Supreme Court supported the lower court.

Caril Fugate was held at the Lincoln State Hospital, a mental institution, and her confinement was much less strict than that for Starkweather. She told the sheriff's wife that she spent her days visiting with other girls in the dormitory and her evenings playing cards, mainly gin rummy, with hospital patients. The newspapers reported she told her attorney she was "not interested" in the Starkweather trial.

She observed her 15th birthday on July 31, 1958, with cake and ice cream and a visit from her stepmother, Mrs. William Fugate, and her sister, Mrs. Barbara Von Busch, who gave her a dress as a gift. In August she was taken to a dentist to have two cavities filled.

Her trial began on Monday, Oct. 27, and there were contrasts with the Starkweather trial:

Only With Eyes Closed Is This Trial The Same

If you sat in the Lancaster District Courtroom I where Caril Fugate is on trial for her life — and closed your eyes for a moment — it could have been the same questions and answers, the same muffled coughing and nervous shuffling of feet, the same sounds and events as occurred last May when her redheaded boyfriend spent his first day in court.

Only one thing was missing: emotion.

The jurors Monday looked on youthful Caril Fugate without the fear, hatred and overwhelmingly curiosity which had greeted Charles Starkweather, and answered the same questions asked by Co. Atty. Elmer Scheele last May without the outbursts of anger of that earlier trial.

Several factors lessened the tension of this second trial, which began in a partially darkened courtroom with the tedious selection of jurors Monday.

For one, time had passed and the hideous events from last Janu-

Caril Fugate's murder trial attracted crowds of reporters and photographers.

ary had passed from the immediate memories of the prospective jury panel members.

And the cocky redhaired youth, whose entrance into the court-house last May brought scores of spectators to view a manacled killer, was not present.

At Caril's entrance into the courthouse, her hand clenched tightly in that of Mrs. Merle Karnopp, the sheriff's wife, she seemed much less like the central figure in a first degree murder trial.

The 15-year-old sat quietly in the courtroom, seemingly swallowed up in the oversized lawyer's chair, with a look of forced attention on her perpetually pouty face.

She was dressed simply in a blue cotton blouse and plaid wool skirt which she might have worn last year when she attended eighth grade classes at Whittier Junior High.

— Star, Oct. 28, 1958

There also was a contrast between the way the Starkweather trial had been reported in the Lincoln newspapers and the way Fugate's was. Charles Starkweather's was page one every day, usually at the top of the page. Caril Fugate's was less prominently reported, although still on the front page. One exception was in the Nov. 5 Star, which carried results of the previous day's election. The Fugate trial story was moved far back in the paper.

On Wednesday, opening statements laid out defense and prosecution contentions:

Lawmen Blamed Caril To Cover Mistakes, Defense Attorney Says

Caril Fugate's defense attorney charged Wednesday afternoon that Lincoln lawmen found it necessary to contend Caril was Charles Starkweather's murder accomplice to cover up their own mistakes.

Atty. John McArthur, in his opening statement at Caril's murder trial in Lancaster District Court, said the 15-year-old girl "did everything in her power" to prevent the murder of Robert Jensen of Bennet. She is charged as Starkweather's accomplice in his death.

Must we condemn Caril, he asked, for failing to do what no one in Nebraska could do: Stop mad killer Starkweather?

McArthur declared that local lawmen "made mistakes" in attempting to solve the Robert Colvert murder (later admitted by Starkweather) which "were repeated" in the later killings attributed to Starkweather.

He did not elaborate on what these "mistakes" were, but did say that police "grossly misinterpreted" Caril's attempts to warn them about Starkweather when they came to her at 924 Belmont.

McArthur also said "police took the position it was none of their business" when told by Caril's friends and relatives of her "strange behavior" when they attempted to gain entrance to her home.

He said from the time Caril came home from school Jan. 21 and allegedly found Starkweather behind the door with a gun in his hand her actions were conditioned by "the vivid memory of a gun pointing in her face."

Caril obeyed Starkweather's instructions implicitly — "just as any other 14-year-old child would do," he added. (Caril was 14 when the crime rampage took place but has since turned 15.)

Lancaster County Atty. Elmer Scheele, however, in his opening statement had a different version of Caril's participation in the murder spree which claimed 10 lives.

Caril "willingly and actively accompanied and assisted Starkweather in the places he went and the things he did," Scheele declared.

She had "ample opportunity" on "more than one occasion" to get get away from Starkweather, he added.

Scheele said, as he did in the Starkweather trial last May, that Caril aided in the robbing and killing of the 17-year-old Jensen. He said Jensen handed Caril his billfold, as ordered, and Caril took the money from it and placed it in Starkweather's billfold.

When Jensen had driven to the abandoned school site east of Bennet as directed by Starkweather, Jensen and his girlfriend, Carol King, were ordered from the car "at gunpoint by both Starkweather and Caril Fugate," Scheele said.

Caril, he said, had a loaded .410 sawed-off shotgun in her possession and Starkweather had a loaded .22 rifle at the time.

Scheele said both Caril and Starkweather, after Jensen and Miss King were shot, attempted to cover up the evidence of the killings (apparently a reference to the cellar being covered up with timber and weeds).

— Star, Oct. 29, 1958

On Thursday eight state witnesses took the stand, but The Star reported: "No new details of the winter crime spree which claimed 10 lives were revealed. Testimony was nearly a carbon copy of that given by the same witnesses at Starkweather's trial last May."

On Friday, a deputy sheriff testified that at the time of her arrest Caril Fugate carried clippings about the murders of the Bartletts; earlier she had said she did not know her family had been killed until after her capture.

But the following Wednesday sparks began to fly at the trial, as Starkweather himself took the stand as a surprise witness for the prosecution:

Starkweather: Caril In Room As Parents Slain

Surprise prosecution witness Charles Starkweather continues his testimony Thursday at 9 a.m. at Caril Fugate's murder trial in

Caril Fugate (center) sits with her defense attorneys in courtroom.

Lancaster District Court.

But Caril probably will be still reeling from her former boy-friend's unexpected appearance Wednesday when, in 2½ hours of testimony, he completely disrupted her claim that she was his hostage on the winter murder spree which claimed 10 lives.

Starkweather, condemned to death in the electric chair but awaiting the outcome of an appeal to the state Supreme Court, shocked the courtroom full of spectators by saying:

— Caril was in the same room as he when he shot her mother, Mrs. Marion Bartlett, and knifed her half-sister, 2½-year-old Betty Jean Bartlett.

— Caril "watched television" while he put the bodies of her family in a chicken coop and abandoned outhouse behind her home at 924 Belmont Jan. 21.

— Caril woke him up the night of Jan. 25 to tell him two police-men were at the door. (She told them the family had the flu and they left.)

— That he, Starkweather, left the Bartlett home on several occa-

Starkweather was a key prosecution witness against Fugate.

sions between Jan. 21 and Jan. 27 (when they left for Bennet) and that Caril stayed behind in the house, alone and not bound.

— That after stopping at Tate's Service Station 8 miles south of Lincoln on U.S. 77 on Jan. 27 for gas, rifle shells and hamburgers, Caril complained the hamburgers "tasted like dog meat" and said "we ought to go back and shoot them."

— That he and Caril stopped at the C. Lauer Ward home at So. 24th Jan. 28 after he "told Caril to pick a place and she picked that one."

— Star, Nov. 6, 1958

The girl's reaction to that testimony caught the reporters' attention:

Witness Starkweather Doesn't Look at Caril;
Fugate Girl Keeps Expression As Ex-Boyfriend Testifies
When Caril Ann Fugate first learned Charles Starkweather was to take the stand against her, her eyes reddened.

She clenched her hands repeatedly.

Her face flushed and her eyes narrowed.

A little later, she looked as if she might have cried during a recess trip to the restroom in close custody of the sheriff's wife.

But when flame-headed Charlie, pale and seemingly confident, came into the courtroom to take the stand, Caril Ann just stared.

She showed interest — or worry — but did not change her expression from the one she's had throughout the trial, though she continued to flush a little.

She did, however, keep one hand on Atty. Merril Reller's arm as she looked past him to the witness chair.

Her hand appeared to rest lightly. It was not clenched, nor her handkerchief wrung, as it had been during the recess.

Charles, condemned to the electric chair for the murder of Robert Jensen, did not look at Caril as he entered the courtroom.

He looked at the judge.

He followed directions to raise his hand, swore to tell the truth, and took the stand.

He seemed to "just miss" seeing Caril, who sits to the left of the bench. (From his own trial, however, he would know exactly where she'd be sitting.)

On the witness stand, though, he naturally faces the defendant.

But he kept his eyes averted.

Part of the time he looked at his feet. Part of the time he had his hand over his face, part of the time he looked at the county attorney, or the court reporter.

He and Caril were never closer than the 20 to 30 feet separating the witness chair and the defendant's seat.

— Journal, Nov. 5, 1958

Another story reported:

> Starkweather also denied that he ever tied or bound Caril be-
> tween Jan. 21st and Jan. 27th when the two were staying at the
> Bartlett home.
> Tears rolled down Caril's face as she listened to a reading of
> Starkweather's statement in which he detailed the killing of the
> Bartletts.
>
> —*Journal, Nov. 5, 1958*

The trial continued for two more weeks, much longer than had Charles
Starkweather's trial. There was abundant conflicting testimony about whether
Caril Fugate had been held hostage, whether she had participated in the slayings, whether she could have escaped. Finally, on Nov. 19, attorneys presented their final arguments:

> **Jury Starts Today; 1st Degree Verdict Sought**
> County Atty. Elmer Scheele Wednesday did not ask the jury to
> impose the death penalty against murder defendant Caril Fugate.
> "I am perfectly satisfied," he said, "to leave the question of the
> penalty up to you."
> Scheele did, however, firmly say he believed the state had
> proved Caril guilty of both the first degree murder and murder
> while in the perpetration of a robbery charge on which she is being
> tried in the Jan. 27 death of Robert Jensen, 17, of Bennet.
> Conviction on either charge is punishable by death or life impris-
> onment at the discretion of the jury.
> The seven men and five women jury members will retire to
> reach a verdict Thursday after being instructed on legal points by
> Lancaster District Judge Harry A. Spencer.
> Scheele, in the final half of his closing argument, lashed out at
> statements made earlier by Defense Atty. John McArthur.
> He accused McArthur of attempting to confuse the jurors by ap-
> pealing to possible prejudices they might have against law en-
> forcement personnel and also of making a "clever appeal" to the
> emotions and sympathies of the jurors instead of discussing the
> facts.
> McArthur had claimed even star prosecution witness Charles
> Starkweather was unable to implicate Caril in the Jensen murder.
> He contended Caril "couldn't possibly" have aided in the Jensen
> killing, which was committed on "impulse" by Starkweather.
> There was no connection, McArthur claimed, between the rob-
> bery of Jensen and his murder.
> McArthur declared that he doesn't believe Scheele or his chief
> deputy, Dale Fahrnbruch, have "ever seen Caril Ann Fugate. I
> think when they look at that chair (where she sits) they see Lucre-

zia Borgia or one of the witches out of Macbeth."

McArthur claimed Lincoln lawmen, being "castigated unmercifully" for failing to apprehend Starkweather, let themselves become engulfed in a cloud of prejudice.

The lawmen, he said, "couldn't believe they had been so stupid. The conviction of Caril Ann Fugate became a must."

Scheele, in reply, countered that McArthur, lacking facts to back up his contention Caril was forced to accompany Starkweather, decided to rely on the adage that "a good offense is the best defense."

Scheele said McArthur then launched attacks on the police, sheriff, sheriff's wife, county attorney and "anybody and everybody" else that suited his purpose — which was to confuse the facts in the case.

Scheele said he called Starkweather to the stand because he is the "only living person who knows what actually happened and what Caril's part was." McArthur had earlier discounted Starkweather's testimony (Starkweather said Caril was his willing companion and helper) as unreliable, and said Starkweather was a "madman, hopelessly insane."

At one point McArthur declared, "I would like to have someone explain to me at what exact moment Caril Ann should have broken and run" away from Starkweather. He said Caril's "physical and mental ability" to escape was gone after Caril saw Starkweather shoot Bennet farmer August Meyer Jan. 27 in cold blood.

Scheele replied that Caril had several opportunities to escape, and said the "best" one was Jan. 25 when two policemen came to her home at 924 Belmont as Starkweather slept.

If Caril had really believed (as she has claimed) that her family was being held somewhere by Starkweather's friends, Scheele said, she would have whispered an appeal to the policemen as Starkweather slept — instead of waking Starkweather up before she answered the door (as she has admitted doing).

Scheele contended Caril would have "grasped" at such a chance for help if she were innocent.

He also said Caril could have given the alarm earlier Jan. 25 when she walked her brother-in-law and sister to a taxi outside her home. Or she could have easily handed a warning note she claims to have written to a service station attendant while Starkweather was in another part of the station (at 17th and Burnham) Jan. 27, Scheele said.

Caril also could have given this note to a waitress at a cafe south of Lincoln later the same day, Scheele said. (Caril ordered hamburgers while Starkweather was in the service station next door having a tire fixed.)

The audience filed out of the courtroom Wednesday without

many backward glances at the young murder defendant. Most of the interest seemed focused on the jurors, and was expressed by one spectator who turned to her friend to remark, "I'm glad I'm not sitting in one of those 12 chairs."

— Star, Nov. 20, 1958

The judge's instructions Thursday allowed five possible verdicts.

Judge's Instructions Specify 5 Verdicts to Be Considered
Seven men and 5 women who hold Caril Fugate's fate in their hands retired to deliberate on a verdict at 10:01 a.m. Thursday.

The jury members, who will not be allowed to separate until a verdict is reached, were to eat their meals at the Lincoln Hotel.

If a verdict is not reached by approximately 10 p.m. Thursday, the jurors will spend the night at the hotel.

The jury retired from the courtroom after hearing District Judge Harry A. Spencer instruct the jury on the law applicable to Caril's case, the possible verdicts they may return.

The possibilities:

1. **Guilty** of the Jan. 27 first degree murder of Robert W. Jensen of Bennet.

2. **Innocent** of Jensen's first degree murder.

3. **Guilty** of murder in the second degree, for which the penalty is 10 years to life imprisonment.

4. **Guilty** of first degree murder "during the perpetration of a robbery."

5. **Innocent** of first degree murder during the perpetration of a robbery.

If the jury returns a guilty verdict on the first-degree count, the jurors must decide if the penalty is to be death or life imprisonment.

— Journal, Nov. 20, 1958

The jury took only a day to debate. Friday's story was a big one — again on page one. And again, for the first time since the murder week, the Journal had to split its city run, which had begun before the verdict was returned. The Journal's headline for the final part of the city edition:

Caril Guilty of First-Degree Murder, Should Get Life—Jury

Young Defendant Sobs After Verdict Is Announced

Gertrude Karnopp escorts Caril Fugate to the Lancaster County courtroom.

And The Star's story the next morning said:

Life Sentence Faces Caril

Ten months to the day after Caril Fugate's family was brutally murdered at 924 Belmont, a Lancaster District Court jury Friday found Caril guilty of a first degree murder charge resulting from the killing rampage which followed.

Caril was convicted specifically of being Charles Starkweather's accomplice in the robbery-murder of Robert Jensen, 17, of Bennet, last Jan. 27. Her attorney said he will appeal the verdict to the state Supreme Court.

The jury recommended life imprisonment for the 15-year-old girl, and this is binding on Judge Harry A. Spencer who will formally sentence her at a later date.

She could have received the death penalty, as did Starkweather, who is now awaiting the result of an appeal to the high court.

It was reported unofficially that the seven men and five women jurors did not take any ballots during their 8 hour, 25 minute consideration of the case Thursday. (They received the case at 10:01 a.m. Thursday.)

The "murder while in the perpetration of a robbery" verdict was reached Friday morning on an early ballot — probably the second. The jurors discussed the case for 1 hour and 5 minutes Friday to bring the total deliberation time needed to unanimously reach a verdict to 9½ hours.

Judge Spencer said the guilty verdict on the murder in a robbery charge alone meant by "inference" that Caril was found innocent of the "first degree murder" charge for which she was also tried in the Jensen death.

It was also unofficially reported the jurors did not even ballot on the "first degree" charge, under which the state would have had to prove Caril knew Jensen was going to be killed before Starkweather shot him. This element of premeditation is not required in the "murder while in the perpetration of a robbery" charge — all which must be proved is that the defendant willingly participated in a robbery which later resulted in the murder of the robbery victim.

First step in the appeal procedure to be followed by defense Atty. John McArthur will be to request Judge Spencer to grant Caril a new trial for "errors" which McArthur will allege ocurred at this trial.

If Judge Spencer overrules this request, as he did in Starkweather's case last May, the conviction will then be taken before the state Supreme Court.

After Caril is formally sentenced to life imprisonment by Judge Spencer — and there was no indication when this will be — she will then be taken to the Women's Reformatory at York, Neb., to begin her term.

Under state law, she must be completely segregated from adult women prisoners until next June 30 when she becomes 16 years of age. Then she will be treated as any other woman prisoner.

Caril broke down and sobbed heavily after hearing District Court Clerk Wilford F. Sanders read the verdict to a nearly full courtroom at 11:09 a.m.

Then, as Judge Spencer addressed the jury, Caril lifted her head from defense Atty. Merrill Reller's shoulder and glared at the 12 jury members for several minutes. She then resumed her sobbing, which could be heard throughout the courtroom.

As she was escorted from the courtroom, still crying, she was asked by the mob of newsmen outside what she thought of the verdict.

"I'm not guilty!" she firmly declared between sobs.

— Star, Nov. 22, 1958

A sidebar to The Star's lead story that day pointed out that Caril Fugate might be paroled at age 31, based on probable commutations and time off for "good time." A 14-year-old sentenced in Nebraska in 1938 for second-degree murder had served 19 years.

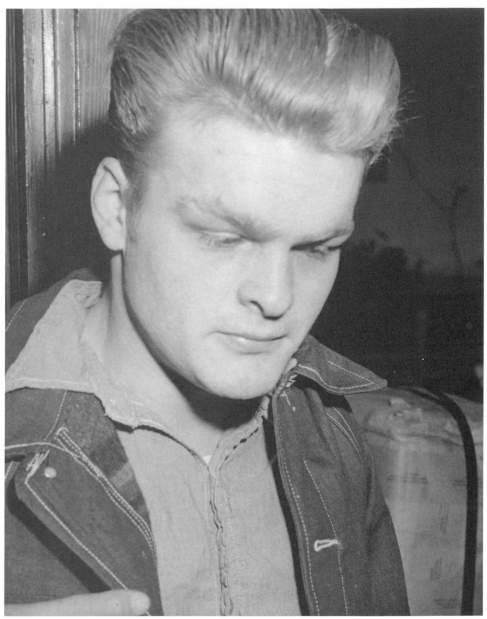

Charles Starkweather spent part of his time awaiting execution at the Nebraska Penitentiary by writing the story of his life.

Murderer's own story

(Reprinted with permission from Parade, © 1959)

On March 15, 1959, the cover of Parade magazine (a publication delivered each week with the Sunday Journal and Star) carried the headline teaser: "Mass murderer Charles Starkweather writes his own story."

For the killer's own story, written while he was in prison awaiting execution, Parade had paid Guy and Helen Starkweather $1,000.

The story began on Page 8 of the magazine with a large picture of Starkweather manacled after his capture in Wyoming and this introduction:

'Bowlegged, redheaded woodpecker'

The kindergarten taunt above stung a 5-year-old on his first day of school. His reaction was to hate.

For 14 years as the boy grew, the hatred smoldered. Finally it touched off one of the most cold-blooded crime sprees in history.

The boy's name: Charles R. Starkweather.

His crime: senseless, aimless mass murder.

The record: 11 dead, including the family of his girlfriend, who accompanied him; responsibility for terror that chilled two states, brought out vigilantes and National Guardsmen, turned the area around Lincoln into an armed camp. Although convicted, his girl friend, Caril Fugate, claims she was only a hostage, not a participant. She now is appealing her life sentence.

His future: on Good Friday, March 27, death in the electric chair.

His story: written, in his own hand, in a bare cell in death row. Before his execution, Starkweather, working feverishly, wants to put on paper the trail of his life from kindergarten to courtroom.

On the next pages, for the first time, highlights from that story are being printed, in his own words. Accompanying it are reports from the few persons who know him best — his parents and a criminologist.

There followed, under the title "A mass killer's handwritten story of a life of REBELLION," three magazine pages of text excerpted and partly edited by Parade from Starkweather's own manuscript:

Around eleven o'clock the night Caril Fugate and I were apprehended, it was very quiet in the Douglas, Wyoming, jail.

I was lying upon the top bunk and was feeling low and hopeless. Then a clear perception of truth came to me of the villainous and outraging acts committed, and I thought I would vomit.

It all seem like a fantastic dream, but it was no dream, and I knew it. Exhausted as I was, I couldn't sleep, I simply laid there, staring at a couple names that had been scratched into the steel wall, and was lost in my own thoughts.

I said to myself, why? Why, why, had everything had to happen to me. I couldn't understand why it seem like ever since my younger days, the whole world was against me. I hated the world with all the poison of a granddaddy rattlesnake ever since I was a youngster, maybe that's why, I thought, it hated me.

Then I was aware that I was lonesome and homesick. I thought of the nice family Sunday picnics and other happy times we all had together.

By this time my head was spinning and whirling, the remembrance of happy times and unpleasant events came crowding through a foggy mist of recollections.

I determined then that I would write these thoughts and remembrances down. For I wanted to do something for my parents. I had caused them enough trouble. And I wanted to warn other boys so they wouldn't take the road I took.

I, Charles Raymond Starkweather, the third child of Mr. and Mrs. Guy Starkweather, was born November 24th, 1938, in a two-story apartment dwelling. But soon my folks secured a seven-room modern home, and I was raised in this house in the south part of Lincoln, Nebraska.

Cowboys and Indians

It seemed like a good childhood. Like almost all other young boys, I was always playing cowboys and Indians with my brothers. We would pick characters such as Daniel Boone, Crazy Horse, Roy Rogers, Lone Ranger and Wild Bill Hickok.

I was five years old when I started kindergarten. The first day, I was filled with excitement and couldn't hardly wait to get there. Dressed in my best Sunday clothes and wearing my new glossy brown shoes that I was so proud of, I lined up with my older brothers and were inspected by Mom's keen eyes for dirt under the fingernails, dirty hands or dirt behind the ears. When she was satisfied, she gave each of us a hug and a kiss on the cheek, and we started off.

My rebellion against the world started the first day in school.

And from that first day I became rebellious. I have stayed in my rebellious mood even to this day. Why? Cause that first day in school I was being made fun at, picked on, laughed at.

Why were they making fun at me? My speech for one thing and the other was my legs. I was a little bow-legged. Maybe that's not much of an excuse to become rebellious. But when people tease, make fun of and laugh at a little youngster in his early childhood, that little youngster is not going to forget it. In those younger years I builded up a hate that was as hard as iron.

As I grew older, my speech defect was overcome. As for my bowlegs, their just as crooked as before. I have never been able to grow out of them and if I have to say so myself, I believe a pig could run between them without touching the sides.

Giggling Girls and Boys

I didn't get along that day in school with the others. They didn't seem to want to have anything to do with me. I played in the sandbox by myself. I glanced at them, the girls giggling and the boys giving off their snickers.

When I arrived home, I tolded Mom of the kids teasing and making fun and that they wouldn't even play with me. And the next day when we went to school, Dad went with us, to talk to the principal.

I was overwhelmed with happiness, thinking that the other kids would talk and play with me after Dad's talk with the schoolmistress. The teacher, Mrs. Mott, first suggested that everyone tell what they did during the summer months. One by one the kids wented before the class. As I sat listening I became more and more anxious to tell of my summer activitys . . . I could tell of good times I had playing with my brothers, tell of all the vegetables I helped Mom can up in jars and going fishing with Dad. I couldn't hardly wait until it was my turn.

But as Mrs. Mott called out my name I felt shy and awkward. As I moved my lips I became nervous and a sob of breath seem to stop in my throat. I was talking very quiet and Mrs. Mott said, "Speak a little louder, Charlie, so everyone can hear you." So I spoked louder and as I did my pronunciation got mixed up and all at once the whole class bursted into laughter.

I goggled around, began to speak again, faint and cracked. The kids bursted into laughter again. I glanced towards Mrs. Mott expecting her to help. Finally, she said, "You may sit down if you like, Charlie." Going back to my seat, I made a solemn vow that I would never stand before another group to make a speech. (I broked it twice, in eighth grade, as president of a Hot Rod Club.)

Then Mrs. Mott explained we would have a recess, and suggested we choose up teams to play kick soccer. At the end of picking the teams there was just one boy that wasn't picked yet. And that boy was a redheaded, bowlegged kid. That boy was I.

Mrs. Mott asked, "Would it be all right with you, Charles, if you would act as a substitute? Would you like that?" I wanted to play kick soccer as well as any other boy. Now that I wasn't going to get to play, my heart droop and sadden, so I slipped out of sight and sat down on the top step of the basement steps.

That was one of the first of my black moods. I sat there and said to myself that someday I'd pay them all back. An overwhelming sense of outrage grew in my mind for a revenge upon the world and its human race.

Back in the classroom, I again had the sandbox all to myself. Finally Mrs. Mott asked me to play somewhere else so others could use the sandbox. When I went to the playhouse, everybody left. Then Mrs. Mott suggested I leave there, too. I never went near either of them again. Finally she brought me watercolor paints and suggested I make my mother a picture. While I was painting I did not pay much attention to others and I finished the painting just as we were ready to go home at the end of the morning.

After I had walked two or three blocks on my way home, I heard giggles and laughter behind me. I glance back over my shoulder and there they were, a half dozen girls and boys making wisecracks about my bowlegs and hair and speech. I could hear them imitating my speech as I kept walking.

The Chorus Begins

I stopped as I came to the next corner and then I heard it for the first time:

"The bowlegged, redheaded woodpecker!

"The bowlegged, redheaded woodpecker!"

A car went by. Another was proceeding from the opposite direction, and I stood waiting for it to pass. By this time every one of the youngsters joined in with the first boy:

"The bowlegged, redheaded woodpecker!

"The bowlegged, redheaded woodpecker!"

All at once the boy that seem to be the leader tooked a couple of steps forward and gave a hardy shove that set me into the streets. The automobile's tires squealed. The car came to a full stop not more than a few feet away. As I got up off the street, the boy that shoved me said, "What happened, bowlegs? Won't those bowlegs hold you up?"

Then he slipped up behind me and jerked the rolled up paper from my hand. It was the painting that I had made for Mom.

They all gathered around and started making wise cracks. My blood was getting steam up and I had a desire to team into them with fists or a stick, brick stone or anything to beat their lousy brains out. But Mom had tolded me the day before not to fight so I dismissed the idea.

Then, as the laughter and giggling began, the leader jeered, "You can't even draw," and tore the painting into little pieces.

I griped my jaw to keep from crying out loud. But it didn't keep the tears from creeping from my eyes and rolling down my cheeks. And then they started in:

"The bowlegged, redheaded woodpecker is a cry baby.

"The bowlegged, redheaded woodpecker is a cry baby."

At that, I turned toward home and ran as fast as my bowlegs would carry me.

That night, Dad phoned someone, I think the principal. I couldn't make out what he was saying, he was talking so fast and so loud. I could tell by the sound of Dad's voice that he was a little disgusted.

When Dad came back into the kitchen he said, "Charlie, from now on if anybody starts picking on you, knock the devil out of them. You won't get a licking from us and if that school trys to because you're fighting for your rights, you just tell your mother."

The next day in school, I received my first fight. The teacher did give me the devil but I didn't tell Mom. I just kept on fighting. The more I was teased, the more I fought. I did a lot of fighting throughout my school years and admit that they were not all cause by being teased. My rebellion against the world became so strong that I didn't care who I fought with or the reason why.

Reputation as a Fighter

I wouldn't deny that I was like a hound dog looking for fights. I would beat them down again until they knew that I wasn't going to take it from them. I fought fast and a little furiously like a maniac in rage and fury.

And when they say that you're a fighter and have a reputation for doing nothing but fighting, then there's going to be a few kids like yourself that are going to try to take that reputation away. My fighting reputation stayed with me throughout my school years and even afterwards.

I gradually did get used to school. It wasn't school I hated, it was the pupils in it. From my younger school days on, I didn't want anything to do with them. So I went off into the woods and forests by myself. Some people would think it would be lonely out in the woods, but it wasn't for me.

I've done quite a bit of hunting and killed quite a bit of game, but I have deep affection for the animals I have killed. No animal is stupid. I well agree they're not all intellect in all respects, but they do know when to hide and when to run.

Many a time, I didn't shoot a game animal, instead I sat motionless, watching their tactics of living in the forest. I've had squirrels come within arm's reach.

Neither my brothers nor I carried a firearm until we were older and knew the safety measures. Dad was an excellent instructor. Firearms besides automobiles have been my ruling passion, but between the firearms and automobiles, I rather hear the crack of a firearm than drive the finest car in the whole wide world.

These years were the most lonely years of my life. Other students wouldn't associate or have much to do with me. For instance, I always gave everyone in the class a Valentine card, but I never received as many back as I gave away. It always disappointed me. The ones I did get I kept for a long while.

What finally made me quit school was hate for other students. After junior high school I did attend a blueprint course at night school and received a diploma. I've often thought, while sitting in my prison cell, of what I would do differently if I could live my life over, and one thing is go all the way through school. As it was, I got a job that didn't amount to beans, and when I tried to get a decent job that had better hours and paid more, I could never get it.

I thought and hoped that the rebellion in my heart, so strong and heavy, would soften or melt or die out when I quit school. But of course it did not.

Sorrow and Remorse

Today, my feelings are of great sorrow and remorse for the people killed. And for the heartache and sorrow and grief caused people who lost their loved ones. I pray that God will be forgiving of what has been done.

My thoughts at the time of the killings was that it was right to protect yourself and kill in self-defense. Some of the victims were killed in that way and others exactly did attempt to block the path of escape.

But today I know that this was wrong. I realize that if I myself was in one of the victims' place, and a murder alarm had gone out then I'd do my best to prevent any escaping, and if my life was going to be taken, I'd fight at all costs and put up one heck of a battle.

All the time the spree was taking place I was scared, jittery, tired from loss of sleep, and very dangerously on edge. At the time I figured I had enough and was going to give up, we were driving back to Lincoln from Bennett. Caril then threatened out loud that she wasn't going to give up, and that I, or no one else was going to make her.

And with a shotgun laying across her lap with the barrel pointing directly at me, and with her fast talking, she convinced me that we didn't have anything to gain by giving up. [This is in accordance with Starkweather's testimony at his trial. — EDITOR]

Love Flourished, Then Died

My feelings toward Caril now are of great regret for ever knowing her. In the past Caril and myself had a lot of good times. Our love in the beginning was very ardent and passionate. But as time went along our love tapered off to emotional passion and then began to fade out. Today my love for Caril is completely dead. I wish it would have ended long before now. But I hold no grudges against Caril.

Today, after a year of imprisonment, I can count my life in hours. I have had a great deal of time for thought and to retrace back over my life. I hold no fear for the electric chair, it is the price I am paying for taking the lives of others. But bringing my life to an end does not answer why certain things took place. Going to the electric chair will bring to an end my search for answers that are hard to find.

Now I feel no rebellion toward anything or anyone, only love and peace. I received this love and peace through the Bible.

And if I could talk to young people today I would tell them to go to school, to go to Sunday school, to go to church and receive the Lord Jesus Christ as your own personal Saviour. Our God is a kind God, He'll forgive and accept you as one of His even if your heart is black and heavy with sin.

And I would say to them to obey their parents or guardians, and stay away from bad influences, and never undertake anything that you don't understand, and if in doubt don't do it. And most of all don't ever let your intentions and emotions overpower you.

If I had followed these simple little rules, as I was advised to do many times, I would not be where I am today.

Fright, anger, investigation

QUESTIONS ARE ASKED

A panic-stricken community reacted with fear and with anger at law enforcement officials early during the Starkweather murder week. Both newspapers asked pointed questions about whether the police had done their job in pursuing the two young killers.

The front page of The Star carried this notice in bold type the day after Charles Starkweather and Caril Fugate were apprehended by Wyoming officials:

> **Police Work Questioned**
>
> Concern has been expressed from some quarters as to the adequacy of the Police Department investigation in the Starkweather case, particularly during its formative stages. The question has been raised whether some of the later killings could have been prevented.
>
> In a story on Page 11, city officials give their answers as to what the early investigation could have been expected to uncover.
>
> *— Star, Jan. 30, 1958*

On the inside page, the story was:

> **Skill Of Law Investigation Here Under Question**
>
> Could the investigative work of law enforcement officers in the Charles R. Starkweather case have been better than it was?
>
> Did the Lincoln Police Department fail to take steps which might have prevented some of the brutal murders of the last two days?

These are questions prominent in the minds of the public as well as city officials. Except from Police Chief Joseph T. Carroll there are as yet no final answers to the questions, but answers are promised from both Mayor Bennett Martin and Welfare and Safety Director Emmett Junge.

The major area of concern involves the time which elapsed between 9:25 p.m. last Saturday when the Police Department investigated a suspicion complaint at 924 Belmont and 4:30 p.m. Monday when three members of the family living at that address were found dead on the premises. Reports show the possibility that the three victims had been dead at the time of the 9:25 p.m. Saturday investigation.

The question then is whether police investigation Saturday and Monday morning before the crime was discovered would have led to earlier discovery of the triple killing. The question is pertinent in that it is assumed that earlier discovery of the murders could possibly have led to apprehension of the killers before they fled Lincoln and snuffed out other lives.

Mayor Martin stated that he and the City Council will secure a complete report on this early phase of the tragedy and make public its opinion as to the adequacy of the investigative work.

"However," Martin said, "I am satisfied from what I know now that nothing more could have been expected from our Police Department for the period through last Saturday night."

In support of this statement, Martin released a full copy of the report made on the Saturday night investigation by the two investigating officers. The report, Martin said, speaks for itself and shows the officers involved acted in the only logical way.

Here the story included the full text of the police report of the Saturday investigation of the Bartlett home, when police, asked by Bartlett relatives to investigate, were turned away by Caril Fugate's statement that members of the family had the flu. The story continued:

Chief Carroll pointed out that at no time until discovery of the bodies was there any indication of foul play.

"We investigate thousands of domestic complaints a month," Carroll said, "and this one appeared to be nothing out of the ordinary. We had no legal right to make a forcible entry into the house and no evidence urging us to do so.

"It is easy to look back now and see what could have been done, but we had no knowledge at the time of anything in the nature of a crime. I fail to see any grounds for criticism of the handling of this investigation."

As to the Monday morning investigation by police, both Carroll and Sheriff Merle Karnopp stated that, while it might seem hard to believe, there was no evidence in the Belmont house to indicate foul play. There were no blood stains and no bullet holes, Karnopp said.

"The complaint was routine," said Welfare and Safety Director Emmett Junge, "and properly investigated. As the statement (of investigating officers on Saturday) shows, the officers were satisfied that the people were sick. At this point, I can see no reason to question the adequacy of the police department work."

Carroll was asked if the officers investigating the complaint Saturday night should have asked to see the reported sick people in the house.

"Not normally," Carroll said, "unless they had some reason to doubt the girl. Even the relatives were apparently satisfied with our investigation and have expressed their surprise at what actually happened."

Mayor Martin said that details of the investigation beyond Saturday night would be thoroughly analyzed by him and the City Council. Until this analysis is completed, he said, it would be impossible for us to give an opinion on the sufficiency of that part of the investigation.

A second complaint from the Bartlett family relatives sent police back to the Belmont home Monday morning. Upon entry into the home, nothing wrong was found and no one found at home.

Carroll was asked if investigating officers Monday should have been suspicious of the empty house in view of a Saturday night report that its occupants had the flu.

"Not necessarily," Caroll said. "It was logical to assume that the sickness was over and the family simply gone."

Carroll was also asked how the murder suspects could elude police for about 48 hours and make their way out of Nebraska and clear to Wyoming.

Carroll answered that every available lead was followed and that the suspects had a good start on an escape by the time each new killing was discovered. Without good pursuit and investigating work, he added, some of the bodies might have not been found yet and the suspects still at large.

— *Star, Jan. 30, 1958*

Later that day, following word from Wyoming indicating that Starkweather had admitted the Dec. 1 murder of Robert Colvert, the afternoon Journal asked pointed questions about the investigation and carried a story about a statement from Starkweather's father:

Starkweather, Officers Comment

Guy Starkweather, father of Charles, commented earlier that "the police could have prevented all this. They had been warned

Saturday night."

He added Thursday to a Journal reporter that "the police had a duty to perform Saturday — they aren't carrying those pistols for nothing."

Starkweather called police Thursday morning denying he had stated anything to the effect that Lincoln police had been inefficient in performing their duty in any part of the crimes recently committed, according to police officials.

Robert Von Busch, son-in-law of Mrs. Bartlett, expressed disappointment in the way the police handled the Belmont matter.

Von Busch said he became worried when he went to the house and was told to leave because the family had the flu.

"So I went down to the police station and told them that something was really wrong at the house," he said. They said that the Bartletts were probably gone on vacation and they were tired of me bothering them all the time."

He continued:

"I knew that something was wrong so I drove back out to the house with Rodney (Charles Starkweather's brother) and checked the back of the house.

"That's when I found the bodies. I then drove back to the police station and told the officers," Von Busch said.

"It sure seems crazy that sick people would go on a vacation leaving a 14-year-old girl behind," Von Busch added.

Police officials comment:

Chief Joseph Carroll — "At no time until the discovery of the bodies in Belmont was there any indication of foul play.

"We had no legal right to make a forcible entry into the house and no evidence urging us to do so.

"I fail to see any grounds for criticism of the handling of this investigation."

Sheriff Merle Karnopp — In Wyoming; couldn't be reached immediately for comment. Earlier said there was no evidence in the Belmont house to indicate foul play. There were no blood stains and no bullet holes, he said.

Nebraska Safety Patrol Director Col. C.J. Sanders — "I was completely satisfied and pleased with the work of my men.

"We didn't put up any physical types of roadblocks (wooden barricade or etc.) because it would have been impossible to cover every route out of Lincoln and the Bennet area with the number of men I had.

"If I would have used my men to set up and maintain roadblocks there would have been no men in the Bennet area to search for Starkweather, who we believed was still there.

"I called into action some 25 troopers and we used them to check farm houses, possible tips, backroads and the highways.

At the Ward murder scene are (from left) Inspector Robert Sawdon, Police Chief Joe Carroll, Lt. Gail Gade, Mayor Bennett Martin and Sgt. Bob Myers.

Welfare and Safety Director Emmett Junge and County Sheriff Merle Karnopp.

"There was no reason to believe that the pair was outside the Bennet area. No report of any other stolen car was received until the couple, then in a 1956 black Packard sedan, Nebraska license 2-17415, was outside of Nebraska.

"All of our some 158 officers throughout the state were alerted by Monday about the Lincoln murders and the missing 1949 Lincoln auto.

"We had a report out immediately to all stations when the Jensen boy's car was missing from Bennet.

"At the time Starkweather was going across Nebraska in the stolen Packard we were still watching for the 1950 blue Ford missing from Bennet.

"It must be remembered that the Nebraska Safety Patrol tries to cover some 10,000 miles of Nebraska highways and roads with only some 158 troopers."

The Patrol official pointed out that there are only two troopers stationed at Broken Bow to cover 200 miles of Sandhill territory toward Alliance.

(It is reported that Starkweather left Lincoln sometime Tuesday night and drove all night across the state, using Highway 2.)

Welfare and Safety Director Emmett Junge — "The complaint was routine and properly investigated. As the statement (of investigating officers on Saturday) shows, the officers were satisfied the people were sick.

"I can see no reason to question the adequacy of the Police Department work."

Det. Ben Fischer, one of the police who went to the Belmont residence on Monday morning — "We went out to the Bartletts at the request of Mrs. Pansy Street, Mrs. Bartlett's mother.

"We entered the house through the window after no one answered at the front door.

"The house was warm and nothing seemed disturbed. Mrs. Street seemed satisfied with the investigation."

Gov. Victor Anderson — "A tremendous job has been done by everyone in this case. I want to commend the alertness of the Wyoming officers for their fine work in apprehending these people."

— Journal, Jan. 30, 1958

That same afternoon the Journal reported about the City Council:

Performance of Lawmen Supported;
City Council Holds a Special Session Covering Police Work

In the wake of "the worst series of murders in Midwest history," the City Council has gone on record unofficially upholding the work of the Lincoln Police Department in their handling of the case.

The action came after citizens began asking questions about law enforcement officials' performance in the case.

Council members Pat Ash, Alfred DuTeau, Dell Tyrell, and Mayor Bennett Martin individually spoke in favor of the work the department did in the case.

Ash said, "The facts before me show no reason for not upholding the police department in this series of crimes."

A poll of the council showed the case for further investigation of the police's handling of the murders wasn't closed.

A councilman said, "Later facts could bring up something which might need additional consideration."

They went on record unofficially.

Chief Carroll told the council the finding of the first three bodies on Saturday might not have stopped Starkweather.

"We have conflicting reports that he was at the house at that time," he said.

Councilman Pat Ash asked Carroll how the size of the police force affected the investigation.

"The size of the present force wouldn't have made any difference up until the first three bodies were found," Carroll replied. "After that we don't know. The more officers we would have had the better the chances to catch him."

— *Journal, Jan. 30, 1958*

Friday morning's Star carried this page one item:

Wyoming Officers Congratulated

Converse County Sheriff Earl Heflin of Douglas, Wyo., received Thursday the following telegram from Walter W. White, publisher of The Lincoln Star:

"I humbly offer to you and your men my sincere thanks for doing a job at which our police force proved inadequate. Our community owes you a real debt of gratitude."

The congratulatory wire referred to the capture of Charles Starkweather by the Wyoming officers.

— *Star, Jan. 31, 1958*

White's telegram and the front page report of it were the more unusual because as publisher and top officer of The Star he virtually never ventured an opinion on news coverage — let alone dictated, as he had, this page one item.

By Friday, public reaction was heating up and the mayor was proposing an investigation. That Friday afternoon's Journal carried a blockbuster copyrighted story by Delbert Snodgrass and Leo Scherer that said several people had given police information that might have linked Starkweather to the Colvert case.

With a two-line, eight-column banner on page one the Journal reported:

4 Say They Gave Tips in December
Linking Starkweather to Colvert Case

At least four Lincolnites say they gave law enforcement officials the name of Charles Starkweather and the description of his car early in December in connection with the Dec. 1 killing of Robert Colvert.

However, both Lincoln police and Lancaster County law officials say Starkweather was never questioned until apprehended in Wyoming by Wyoming law officials.

— Journal, Jan. 31, 1958

The Journal story then quoted:

■ The operator of a clothing resale store as saying she reported to police a description of Starkweather as a person who had paid for about $10 in purchases with coins.

■ An attendant at a gas station on Highway 77 south of Lincoln who saw a shotgun in the car of a youth who bought gasoline and shells on Monday.

■ The manager of the service station where Colvert worked, saying both a former employee of the station and an employee of a business across the street had provided descriptions of Starkweather as a person who had been hanging around the station, as well as a description of Starkweather's car.

The balance of the story did not, however, detail any instance of Starkweather's name being mentioned to law enforcement officials. The Star's lead story the next morning also reported the descriptions given to police in the Colvert case, but they stated that Starkweather had not been named to officers.

Lancaster County Attorney Elmer Scheele stepped into that controversy the next day with a statement reported in the Saturday Journal:

Information Didn't Link Starkweather, Colvert

None of the information developed during the course of the investigation of the Robert Colvert case "led any of us to realize Charles Starkweather was involved," Lancaster Co. Atty. Elmer Scheele said Saturday.

He made the statement at a gathering of law enforcement officials in his office.

Scheele commended the authorities for their work in the investigation of the Dec. 1 Colvert slaying.

"However, due to public statements that have been made," he said, "it seems to me that it is necessary for us, in the public interest, to interrupt our investigation at this point long enough to correct some misconceptions that have been given to the public."

Scheele added he has "never seen any more efficient or more devoted law enforcement officials than we have in Lincoln and Lancaster County."

— Journal, Feb. 1, 1958

Stories also were beginning to appear about such issues as the size of Lincoln's police force. The Friday afternoon paper's front page reported:

Police Manpower Lack Cited

Police Chief Joseph Carroll has said repeatedly that the Lincoln police force is seriously hampered from carrying out the duties required for a city the size of Lincoln because of the lack of manpower and huge turnover of the commissioned officers.

According to police statistics, the department now has 92 commissioned officers compared to the authorized strength of 95 as allowed by a budget set by the city council.

The most recent Uniform Crime Reports published by the FBI says that cities the size of Lincoln have 1.9 police officers to every thousand persons according to national average, which means that if Lincoln were average the city would have 243 police officers compared to the present force less than half that size.

The National Safety Council said that Lincoln needed at least 80 more police officers.

According to Carroll's earlier statements, the shortage of men is not the department's only manpower problem, "because inadequate salaries make a police service training program necessary to be carried on all the year around, our service time to the public is cut down seriously."

Carroll has said that one experienced officer is worth two recuits and the police have worked with inexperienced men in many instances where they could not efficiently perform their duties.
— *Journal, Jan. 31, 1958*

The report of a shortage of manpower was not a new complaint. The day before the Bartletts' bodies were found, the Sunday Journal and Star had carried a story saying 30 policemen had left the department in the previous 18 months. "However," that story noted, "police officials said there were no unsolved major crimes in the city in 1957."

On the Friday after the killings, Mayor Bennett Martin was promising continued investigation and said that he would forward reports to the City Council when law enforcement officers returned from Wyoming.

Before the day was done, the mayor had decided on a further step.

Independent Probe Talked By Mayor

Mayor Bennett Martin has announced he will propose that the City Council investigate the possibility of hiring an outside firm of experts "in this particular field" to clear up doubt which may exist in connection with the investigation of the Colvert murder.

In a report listed late Friday Mayor Bennett Martin said:

"In view of the high sentiment prevailing in regards to the adequacy of the Police Department investigation of the Starkweather case, I am proposing that the City Council investigate the possibility of hiring an outside firm of experts in this particular field to clear up any doubts which may exist in connection with the investigation. I believe this to be essential for the well being and peace of Lincoln and in fairness to the Police Department.

"I have already acted to obtain all the facts in connection with reports that law enforcement officials had notice of Starkweather's implication in the Colvert murder at the time of commission of this crime and failed to adequately use this information.

"I had planned a family trip to visit my daughter, who resides in California, but in view of the public concern on issues involved in the Starkweather case I have cancelled my plans for the trip in order to give personal attention to every important detail facing the community on this subject."

— Journal, Jan. 31, 1958

It didn't take the City Council long to respond. By Monday afternoon this council action was reported in the Journal:

City Council Agrees On Full Investigation

The Lincoln City Council has unanimously agreed to a full investigation of police handling of the recent murder cases in Lincoln.

"The purpose of the investigation is to find where we're wrong, if we're wrong," Mayor Bennett S. Martin said.

"It's a bad situation when the people don't have faith in their police department."

"This investigation should clear up any doubt that the people have, and if the investigation disloses any failure, positive action will be taken by the City Council," he said.

Martin said the number of persons to head the study hasn't been decided but when a decision is reached, "the entire program will be made public."

"The main purpose of the investigation is to clear up any doubt that may exist in the minds of the people for the welfare of the community, the peace of mind of the citizens and in fairness to the Lincoln Police Department," he said.

He said the Council and Lancaster County Commissioners will meet at 2 p.m. Tuesday to "review with the county some of the local thinking on the matter."

Mayor Bennett S. Martin had announced earlier that he would ask the council to consider hiring an outside firm of experts "in this particular field" to clear up doubt which may exist in connection with the investigation of the Colvert murder.

— Journal, Feb. 3, 1958

By Tuesday afternoon, the city and county had joined in a full-scale investigation. Their action was reported in Wednesday's Star:

County And City Join In Probe Of Slaying Case

Lincoln and Lancaster County joined Tuesday for a "full and thorough" investigation of police and county law enforcement agencies in the handling of the Colvert murder and the Charles Starkweather mass slayings.

The City Council and County Board agreed to a plan by which a three-man committee would pick an investigator.

Mayor Bennett Martin named James Ackerman, local attorney and former FBI man, as city member of the committee, and County Board Chairman Russell Brehm announced another ex-FBI man, auto dealer J. William Mowbray, as the county's member. The two will pick the third member of the committee.

— Star, Feb. 5, 1958

Both members of the committee were important local civic leaders connected with major business interests. Ackerman was general counsel for Bankers Life Insurance Co. and county Republican chairman. Mowbray was president of Mowbray Motors Inc.

The two men chose for the third member of the committee another representative of Lincoln's power structure, Dwight C. Perkins, an attorney and president of Farmers Mutual Insurance Co. He was cited as having had "extensive investigative experience" during a five-year U.S. Army career. The only dissent about the committee's membership noted in the newspapers came from the local Democratic county chairman, who questioned whether it was appropriate for the Republican county chairman to serve.

On Feb. 24 the committee named its investigator. The Journal's report that day:

California Investigator Picked

Harold G. Robinson of Burlingame, Calif., a former FBI agent and prominent investigator, has been selected jointly by the City Council and Lancaster County Board to make the full scale review of law enforcement handling of the Charles Starkweather slayings.

The selection came Monday morning after a special three-member Lincoln committee recommended Robinson to the Council and County Board.

Robinson now is the deputy director of the Division of Criminal Law and Enforcement in the California Department of Justice. He is also instructing advanced criminal investigation at the University of California School of Criminology.

The Council and County Board agreed to pay Robinson $100 a day plus expenses for his work in Lincoln which is estimated to take from one to two weeks.

James Ackerman, city member of the committee, told the Council that the recommendation of Robinson was "the highest of any of the persons considered by the committee to come to Lincoln at this time."

The three-member committee of Ackerman, J. William Mowbray and Dwight C. Perkins commented that Virgil Peterson, director of the Chicago Crime Commission, and James W. Connor, director of the St. Louis Crime Commission, had both recommended Robinson as "an able and conscientious investigator who was well versed in investigative techniques."

County Board Chairman Russell Brehm said he felt Robinson should be responsible to the committee and not to the city or county when he conducts the investigation.

"He (Robinson) should be responsible to someone while he's here," he declared.

Commissioners Rollin Bailey and Del Lienemann agreed that the public should not feel the investigator will "whitewash" the probe.

In announcing their selection, the three-member committee noted Robinson had "extensive investigative and criminal experience" since entering law enforcement work in 1934.

From 1934 to 1941, Robinson served with the Federal Bureau of Investigation as a special agent, serving in Birmingham, Atlanta, Memphis and New York City. He was assistant agent in charge of the FBI's New York field office.

During his FBI experience, Robinson investigated all types of federal criminal offenses, including several famous kidnapping cases, according to the three-member Lincoln committee.

The California crime expert was also assigned by FBI Director J. Edgar Hoover to special cases during the early part of World War II.

These special cases included espionage involving the Gustave Gunether Rumrich and Fritz Joubert Duquesne cases. (The cases were later dramatized as "Confessions of a Nazi Spy" and "The House on Ninety-second Street.")

Robinson served as chief investigator with the Truman Committee of the U.S. Senate investigating the national defense program and later as chief investigator of the Kefauver Senatorial Committee investigating organized crime in interstate commerce.

— *Journal, Feb. 24, 1958*

Robinson announced he planned to begin his work in Lincoln about March 10. He actually started March 11, and at the time set an "outside limit of two weeks" for his investigation. His report was made public 11 days later.

EXONERATION OR WHITEWASH?

The main headline on the front page of the Sunday Journal and Star for March 23 read:

'No Laxity' Is Report
On Starkweather Case

And this was the story, by a Journal crime reporter:

The special investigator hired to study the handling of the Charles Starkweather case reported Sunday he found no law enforcement laxity.

Harold G. Robinson's findings were outlined in a 43-page report to city and county officials.

He said he uncovered "no laxity" in the investigation of the Robert Colvert murder case or the handling of police calls at the Marion Bartlett home Jan. 27.

The report contained no discrepancies about the handling of the triple Bennet slaying or the three murders at the C. Lauer Ward residence.

"Fate played its hand a number of times," Robinson said in commenting on Starkweather's successive evasion of the all-out law enforcement search.

The investigator said it was his opinion that the investigation of the Colvert murder "was not inadequate in any material respect."

Regarding two visits to the Bartlett home by police before the three bodies were found, Robinson said the police were sent as a "patrol duty" and not on an investigation.

"This was the most unorthodox pattern of crime that I have ever investigated," Robinson said. "He had the breaks all the way."

The former FBI officer, now with the California Department of Justice, said Starkweather "used a certain amount of cunning" to cover up his tracks.

One of Robinson's strongest recommendations was for local and county officials to come up with something to "cope with panic if it should happen again."

He said that public hysteria which prevailed — house-to-house searches, roadblock demands, citizens carying guns — were all "extremely dangerous."

Robinson said his investigation consisted of a check of all law enforcement records on the case and personal talks with all main individuals who had something pertinent to contribute.

Robinson's report had this to say about the Colvert case: "The investigation of the Colvert slaying by the law enforcement agencies wasn't inadequate in any material aspect. . . . They took the necessary steps which were dictated by the meager information made available to them by residents of the area, who now find a deeper significance.

"It can be cited that until his apprehension in Wyoming, the name of Charles Starkweather didn't enter into the investigation of the Colvert murder."

Among his other recommendations, Robinson urged that a police officer be assigned to the county sheriff and a deputy assigned to the police force as a coordinating move.

One of the most serious things affecting the Lincoln police force, he said, "is its large turnover." Robinson urged favorable consideration of higher salary adjustments.

Robinson said he couldn't see any major disadvantage of "greater cooperation" between the city and county law enforcement agencies. The investigator said the "difference of jurisdiction" between the city and county was a hindrance in having a joint, city-county investigative office.

Law enforcement agencies, the report said, did all possible in the Colvert case, considering there were no latent prints and considering the withholding of information from authorities.

"Much criticism has been voiced concerning the reason the officers didn't inquire as to the identity of the doctor attending the Bartletts," the report continued.

"Perhaps under ideal circumstances of experience and training an officer would make such an inquiry, but it is my own opinion that in the absence of any circumstances which might have prompted the officers to suspicion the conduct of Caril Ann Fugate, of the explanation she offered, such interrogation would not necessarily follow and the officers are not subject to criticism for their oversight when a careful review is made of the attending circumstances."

Why did the officers fail to search the outbuildings at the Bartlett home?

In his report, Robinson said, "In the light of subsequent developments it is regrettable that they did not, but it must be borne to mind that the prime reason for them going to the premises was not to conduct a search, but to satisfy Mrs. Pansy Street concerning the subject matter of her complaint."

Robinson told the officials that Mrs. Street told him she was satisfied after the investigation by the two police officers and herself.

The report said the police radio log indicated radio alerts were broadcast as soon as information came into possession of enforcement agencies.

— *Sunday Journal and Star, March 23, 1958*

A second story on the page, by The Star's police reporter:

> Investigator Harold Robinson said it was regrettable that persons who it later developed had important information concerning the Robert Colvert murder did not turn this information over to lawmen.
>
> The prime example, he said, was a comment made by Charles Starkweather's brother, Rodney, immediately after the bodies of the Marion Bartlett family were discovered Jan. 27.
>
> "I . . . own a 12 guage shotgun that I loaned to my brother in November and he returned it to me after the Robert Colvert murder," Rodney Starkweather reportedly told police.
>
> "Had this information been given to the investigating authorities during the course of the Colvert inquiry the immediate effect is so obvious as to require no comment," Robinson said in his report.
>
> Robinson said that if the personnel of the Crest Station had only done what Co. Atty. Elmer Scheele had asked them to do — tell authorities any fragment of information about persons who frequented the station regardless of how important it may seem — Starkweather might have been linked to the Colvert killing.
>
> Robinson said "much further investigative work and tragedy could have been avoided" if three Crest employees had only recalled that Starkweather frequented the station, often helping the night attendant and sometimes sleeping in his car parked nearby.
>
> One attendant, Robinson stated, now recalls that he had even complained because Starkweather looked over his shoulder late one night while he (the attendant) was balancing the cash receipts.
>
> Starkweather and Caril also went to the Crest Station for gas after leaving the Bartlett home Jan. 27 and their car was serviced by the same attendant who had complained about Starkweather looking over his shoulder, Robinson said.
>
> Robinson said Starkweather and Caril Fugate went into the Crest Station about one week after the Colvert murder. Caril reportedly examined a toy doll before she and Starkweather left.
>
> Robinson said an attendant at Crest did tell a deputy sheriff about a young redhead with a peculiar walk, "as though he had straddled a barrel," who hung around the station.
>
> The attendant, however, said he did not know the youth's name, only that he drove a 1941 Ford (Starkweather had traded this for a 1949 Ford before the Colvert killing).
>
> Robinson also commented on information given police by Mrs. Katherine Kamp, a clothing store operator, who said a youth, later identified as Starkweather, bought $9.95 worth of clothing after the Colvert murder.
>
> But Robinson said "the identification actually given by the woman was of a male, unkempt individual, approximately 25 to 30

years of age.

"In connection with this incident it is cited that the police made prompt follow-up by exhibiting photographs of possible suspects, but here again fate intervened in favor of Charles Starkweather, and it can only be cited that the police had no photograph in their files resulting from any previous violations of law on his part," Robinson said.

— Sunday Journal and Star, March 23, 1958

Robinson offered only six criticisms:

1. **Inadequate appropriation** in city and county budgets for operation of police and sheriff's office.

2. **Some individuals** connected with the case had pertinent information which wasn't passed on to autorities. This included those who discovered the Colvert body and personnel of the Crest Service Station.

3. **Need for more mutual understanding** between the citizens and the law enforcement agencies.

4. **Need for higher salary adjustments.**

5. **Large turnover** within police department.

6. **Need for centralization** of some records and identification of the Lincoln Police Department, Lancaster County Sheriff's Office and the Nebraska Safety Patrol.

— Sunday Journal and Star, March 23, 1958

Local police officials could not have been happier. The paper reported:

Authorities: 'Clean Bill'

Local authorities have expressed approval of Harold Robinson's investigation into the handling of the Charles Starkweather murder case.

Those available for comment agreed that Robinson made a thorough and unbiased report.

Mayor Bennett Martin said he was "terrifically impressed" with the report and added he felt the investigation gave the Lincoln Police Department "a clean bill of health."

Martin said the council will now make a thorough study of the recommendations Robinson made.

County Board Chairman Russell Brehm said he was satisfied the report was an unbiased one.

Co. Atty. Elmer Scheele recalled an earlier statement in which he said he had never seen a more efficient law enforcement group "with the resources at their disposal."

Police Chief Joe Carroll said he was "very happy" Robinson came to the conclusion that authorities had done "everything in their power" to bring the murder cases to a conclusion.

Sheriff Merle Karnopp said he was "naturally pleased" with the report "of a man of Robinson's experience."

Col. C.J. Sanders, head of the Safety Patrol, was out of town.

— *Sunday Journal and Star, March 23, 1958*

Among the general public, those interviewed the next day had varied opinions, ranging from "I think we wasted $1,300 and expenses" to "I think he did just what the police told him to do. I'd do that too for $100 a day" to "I thought it was a very fine report."

In following days other parts of the investigator's report found their way into print, including this story in the Journal on March 24:

> Investigator Harold Robinson has questioned the feasibility of calling out the National Guard, Sheriff's Posse and others carrying guns during the recent Starkweather episode.
>
> "These actions were taken on the spur of the moment," Robinson said, "without anyone thinking of the possible consequences."
>
> The investigator, reached in California by telephone, said the city and county officials should get together and "come up with something to cope with panic if it should happen again."
>
> Robinson termed the public hysteria which prevailed in Lincoln as "extremely dangerous" especially the house-to-house searches, roadblock demands and unauthorized people carrying guns.
>
> He said these questions — Who will be armed? Where should roadblocks be set up? Who should call out additional personnel? and Who should direct the operation? — should be answered after a "long look."
>
> "Where is the line of responsibility?" Robinson asked. "This is the most important question which would have to be decided."
>
> The investigator said different division of responsibility in combined law enforcement "wasn't good."
>
> — *Journal, March 24, 1958*

And this story appeared in The Star that day:

> **Turnover Rate Hurts Quality**
>
> The Lincoln Police Department has had an 86.3% personnel turnover during the past five years.
>
> This handicap was cited by Harold Robinson in commending the excellent record of the department in solving 13 out of 13 murders and five of six manslaughter cases during the past 10 years.
>
> His tabulation showed 82 separations from an authorized force of 95. Present strength is 92.
>
> "More significant than the excessive turnover," he said, "is the fact that 48.6% of those men lost . . . were those having more than

two years of experience, viz: the more experienced men."

Robinson said, "This fact would not, in and of itself, be significant if there existed within the department an adequate training program for new recruits and for in-service training of the established force."

Robinson criticized the police training program as consisting of only two weeks' in-service training school every January.

— Star, March 24, 1958

City and county officials were restrained in their comments — the report would get serious study, they said. In August 1958, beginning police pay was raised 6 percent, but no mention of the Starkweather case was made.

Two years later, The Star's police reporter looked into what changes had occurred as a result of the Robinson recommendations. He reported:

■ No citizen's advisory committee on crime prevention had been appointed and neither Sheriff Merle Karnopp nor Police Chief Joe Carroll believed such a committee was necessary.

■ No full-time exchange of personnel had begun, although one officer from each department had been assigned to work together on major cases.

■ Three men had been given FBI Police Academy training and a fourth was planned, as Robinson had recommended.

■ Police reported training had been improved, but no "officer of superior rank" had been assigned to the task, and the officer assigned had had only limited training.

■ Beginning police salaries had been boosted nearly 20 percent.

Later, in 1960, the Lincoln City Council authorized a 10 percent increase in Police Department strength.

Community failure

Charles Starkweather's and Caril Fugate's victims had not been dead a week before Lincoln community leaders began to ask publicly whether the case revealed failure on the part of the people and agencies of the community:

Ministers Ask That City Ponder Responsibility In Slaying Case

Lincolnites were asked Sunday to ponder the responsibility of this community, its schools and its churches in the Charles Starkweather tragedy last week.

Several local ministers spoke to their congregations on this theme.

"We are all tied together in this sorrow," Dr. Frank A. Court told the congregation of St. Paul Methodist Church, and should question just where we come in, and how we might have done more to prevent a boy to go so far astray.

"These two youths (Charles Starkweather and Caril Fugate) are products of our community and we all have to share responsibility that we didn't reach out and help them with a higher line of thinking and action," he commented.

Commenting on the part of the church, Dr. Court said, "Here was a boy who lived only a few blocks from this church," yet he had never been brought into the fellowship of the church.

"I, too, as head of the City Council's Juvenile Crime Prevention Committee, must share in the sense of responsibility," Dr. Court added.

"All of us have lived through a harrowing week, a week which the thinking people of Lincoln will not forget for a long time," Dr. Frederick Roblee told the congregation of Westminster Presbyterian Church.

"These young people, of course, are responsible for what they did," Dr. Roblee said, "but some of the blame must also be shouldered on many others. All of us in fact, must share in the responsibility of allowing false standards and values deeply to condition today's youth."

Comments of other Lincoln ministers:

Dr. Carl Davidson, pastor of First Methodist Church: "We should be wondering where the community, the home and the church had failed." Anyone, he said, who felt that to "be somebody" he had to be a criminal, reflects a serious lack in our society.

— *Star, Feb. 3, 1958*

By the end of that week, a local minister who headed a youth agency was urging treatment for potential problem children not yet delinquent:

Why Wait Until Child Displays Delinquency?

Neither Charles Starkweather nor his 14-year-old girlfriend had been recognized as particular behavior problems before Lincoln's recent murderous tragedy.

If they had been?

The schools and private agencies offer some help for maladjusted children, but, in a special statement released by Chairman C. Vin White, the executive committee of the Lincoln Youth Project feels that the city needs "a program of early recognition and treatment of serious maladjusted children."

The recent tragedy in our community particularly emphasizes this need, Dr. White said.

And he noted, "there are no psychiatric clinics in this town."

Treatment even of pre-schoolers with serious problems needs to be provided, the project chairman explained.

(Researchers have found that a large number of delinquents had earlier shown a persistent behavior pattern indicating something was wrong.)

In the statement, Dr. White continued: "The committee recognizes that all cases of maladjustment among children cannot be corrected even if located in the early stages.

"However, the committee also realizes the importance of recognizing maladjustment in young children and the part it plays in the prevention of later, more serious emotional disturbances or mental illnesses."

— *Journal, Feb. 8, 1958*

That story and a more detailed one on an inside page were written by Marj Marlette, a Journal reporter who was to write about Charles Starkweather and Caril Fugate for many years. The story on the inside page:

Journal reporter Marj Marlette.

Child Recognized as 'Disturbed' — What Then?

What happens if a child is pinpointed as a disturbed personality?

What facilities does Lincoln have for initially recognizing and treating such problems?

Charles Starkweather had never been a noticeable problem. He caused "some difficulties," but he was not even reported to the school's guidance office for misbehavior before he left school after completing the ninth grade.

Caril Fugate, an eighth-grader at Whittier Junior High, was not only not a problem, but her school deportment was considered "good."

At present, what facilities does Lincoln have to deal with potential delinquency?

Most important contact with any child over five years of age is through the schools.

In the Lincoln Public Schools, according to officials, every youngster is given regular intelligence and achievement tests.

While these may call attention to personality difficulties, more likely — as in the cases of Starkweather and Miss Fugate — they will show if a child is mentally slow and needs special classwork. It is, therefore, usually up to the individual teachers to notice exceptional behavior and personality patterns that need help.

Once observed by the teacher, a child may be sent to the school guidance office, and may be given psychiatric and psychological tests to determine what mental or emotional disorder is present — or if any is present.

A part-time psychiatrist, Dr. Janet Palmer, serves the school three half-days a week. Psychologist Janet Smith works full time for the schools, and Child Welfare Worker Ellamae Reimers and Attendance Coordinator Zora Tennant both do full-time case work. Work of the home-bound teachers may also partially fall in the field of social case work.

In addition to their own staff, the schools receive testing help from the Psychological Clinic at the University of Nebraska when necessary.

The University clinic is a training unit for graduate students in clinical psychology.

After the schools have discovered a problem and diagnosed its probable cause and best program for treatment, it's up to the parents to follow through and get that help.

If parents will accept help?

Recommendations for treatment may include reference to the Child Guidance Clinic, or the University of Nebraska Psychlogical Clinic, or to a private psychiatrist. (No direct referral is made, however. The parents must take the next step themselves.)

Private psychiatric help is arranged for and paid for entirely by the parents.

At the Child Guidance Clinic, a private agency, costs are based on the family's ability to pay and cases are "never turned down because a family can't pay," Stanley Good, director of the clinic, explained.

Children's problems may also become known through their contact with police.

If a child is brought to juvenile authorities by police, he or she may be taken to the University of Nebraska Psychological Clinic even before being taken to court, if an emotional disturbance is apparent. This clinic's services are used extensively, Mrs. Helen Cox, chief juvenile probation officer, said.

The juvenile office can also make use of the public schools' psychological and psychiatric testing services, the Child Guidance Clinic, and the State Hospital.

Once diagnosed, treatment, if needed, can be required by a Juvenile Court order.

— Journal, Feb. 8, 1958

The most complete attempt by the papers to cover this aspect of the case appeared beginning Feb. 13, a six-article series by Star reporter Nancy Benjamin, who would continue to cover various aspects of the murder case until, years later, she moved to reporting jobs in San Diego and then The Los

Angeles Times, from which she is now retired. The series is repeated below here its entirety:

The Starkweather Murder Case ... Why ...
What Could Have Prevented It ... What Can Be Done Now?

Why did he kill?

The startling answer to that question is the lack of an answer. Charles Starkweather killed 11 persons and yet his community, his family, his companions and co-workers, his former teachers, must honestly admit there was no apparent reason for his crimes.

After the capture, and after recriminations and accusations die down, other questions arise which might have answers more important to the community.

The case of Charles and Caril is now in the hands of jurors and judges, but the problem of other teen-agers who may meet the same life circumstances — and react differently or in the same way as Charles — remains in the hands of the community.

Why was Charles not recognized as a potential killer during his 19 years of life in Lincoln?

Were the juvenile, educational and governmental agencies of Lincoln lax in not recognizing this youth as a potential danger?

Will this happen again?

Could these crimes have been prevented?

Are we, as a community, facing up to the problem of juvenile delinquency? (Juvenile delinquency seems a mild phrase to use in connection with Charles Starkweather.)

Does it take 11 murders to jolt us out of the feeling that Lincoln is a better place than any other community with juvenile delinquency and crime problems?

Where have we failed and — more important — what can we do about it?

The opinion that "we have failed somewhere" has been voiced from many Lincoln pulpits and in the public letters of newspapers, along with the sentiment that "we must do something."

Many other communities have faced youthful crime waves — although rarely as gruesome or inexplicable — and have asked the same questions and expressed the same sentiments.

Some of these cities have held protest meetings and civic gatherings to place blame or seek out the faults of their community programs dealing with youth.

Others, perhaps more realistically, sought outside help for a survey of prevention and correction methods of handling youthful crime problems.

Still other towns have waited until the black headlines and lurid details subsided and passed individual judgment on the offenders as "dope addicts or drunks," "products of a poor home," or "one kid in a million . . . this will never happen again." And then forgotten the crime.

One strange facet of the Charles Starkweather case is that Charles himself was not a juvenile delinquent. Yet, his murder spree focused the attention of Lincoln on the problems of juvenile delinquency.

Starkweather had no juvenile criminal record, no truancy or discipline record in school, no contact with youth agencies, welfare groups or juvenile authorities. Any or all of these groups might have aided him or prevented him from committing murder . . . if they had reached him.

The first step leading to a better city program of dealing with maladjusted and delinquent youth is the assessment of what the community has and what the community needs.

The question, "Why was Starkweather never reached by those who might have helped him?" is closely connected with this first step.

Many Lincoln juvenile workers have expressed their opinions privately on this question, but declined public comment, which might endanger their positions or agencies or offices.

A majority of juvenile authorities agree that too much finger-pointing could be construed as direct comment by one group on the lack of another. Yet all agree that the facts should be known to the people of Lincoln who, as taxpayers and donors of time and money, will pay the costs of an adequate, above-average system of youth adjustment and youth crime prevention and correction.

Citizens have the right to know the situation as it stands, the remedies suggested by authorities in the field, and the cost.

The following articles will be an attempt to report the opinions of Lincoln officials now dealing with juveniles as well as the opinions of national authorities.

But the cause of any lessons learned by Lincoln citizens and the central figure in this series is Charles Starkweather, 19.

— Star, Feb. 13, 1958

Visiting Counselor At Schools
Might Have Aided Confused Starkweather

Charles Starkweather spent 11 of his 19 years attending Lincoln schools. Some critics say this indicates that Charles' behavior is therefore 11/19ths the fault of the schools.

But let's look at the facts.

Charles started kindergarten at Saratoga School. He was chunky, bowlegged, freckle-faced and took turns at being silent and belligerent.

He didn't like circle games where he had to join hands with the children on either side of him. He would stand off to the side and watch, and seemingly be contented doing so.

He didn't respond quickly, and sometimes not at all, to the teacher's instructions to the class or to him personally.

Saratoga School officials reported no truancy or discipline problems with Charles in his stay from kindergarten through fifth grade. They recognized his capacities early, even before he was required to repeat the third grade because of his inability to pass reading tests.

Ear trouble, diagnosed as abscesses, was first discovered by a teacher, then reported to the school nurse, who in turn informed his parents.

Due partly to his IQ — which was below the average range of 90 to 110 — and partly to his unresponsiveness, Charles was placed in special classes where the frustration of competing with much brighter students was removed.

Charles was lucky. If he had been born a few years earlier, these classes would not have been available. It is a relatively new and important innovation in the school system of Lincoln.

In his last year of grade school — sixth grade — his family moved and Charles attended Clinton School. Here he again was placed in special classes, where his performance was good to average and his citizenship fair. At the end of the year, he was moved up to junior high school on a "special adjustment" basis, and given an attendance certificate to show he had attended if not graduated formally from grade school.

He started junior high at Irving with a special permit because he lived outside the school area. He told his folks, "I like the gang out there better." School officials agreed because Irving Junior High was not overcrowded and some special attention could be given to Charles.

After completing the seventh and eighth grades without any major discipline problems which would have caused his expulsion, Charles transferred to Everett Junior High for ninth grade.

The Irving "kids" said he left "because he was always picking fights." Charles did get into fights. He went at "bigger guys" with his fists and knees, and once, the kids say, with a knife.

If you pin them down, the kids, now young adults, admit that many of the fights were set up and that Charles was taunted with nicknames like "Pinky" and "Speckles" and "Baby Red" until he jumped at the nearest taunter.

"Who shot your horse?" was a popular teen-age phrase referring to Charles' bowleggedness.

School authorities had no legal right to stop fights off the school grounds or to punish the fighters. Besides, kids stick together and protect the fighters after a battle. School authorities knew about the fights.

There are many clues in Charles' school behavior which, in retrospect, become clear symptoms of maladjustment and point out his "pre-delinquent behavior."

His teachers may have recognized and attempted to cope with these danger signs outlined as signals of maladjustment by authorities:

Fearfulness, timidity and withdrawal; sullenness and resentfulness; inability to get along with other pupils; telling fantastic stories; bullying, quarreling, fighting; temper tantrums; excessive daydreaming; inability to accept authority; tendencies to take refuge in symptoms of complaints of illness when confronted with difficult situations; nervous mannerisms.

How did Charles fit these patterns? He was not a classic example of pre-delinquent behavior but even behind his shield of silence and indifference, his teachers knew that "something was wrong."

Some tried to reach him, giving him special jobs of cleaning the blackboard, checking attendance, or later, running the school movie projector. Some tried to find out what his interests were and to help him develop them.

Teachers tell of his bursts of enthusiasm, soon over, for special assignments. The energy and interest was soon gone, turning to seeming boredom or disinterest. Perhaps he wanted more important jobs or perhaps he was afraid he might fail, they relate.

No teacher referred Charles to the school psychologist because his behavior was not interfering with school routine; his problems at times seemed to be ones of just growing up. (The school system has a school psychologist, plus a Lincoln psychiatrist called in for special cases.)

Charles' behavior patterns, according to national surveys of maladjustment, probably changed very little between the ages of 7 and 12, but the chances of checking his maladjustment grew slimmer each year he came nearer adolescence.

The best time to recognize and treat the pre-delinquent is between the ages of 5 and 10. In some cities, a system of "early recognition" of potentially dangerous symptoms is a reality, but for Lincoln it is still a dream not yet implemented with necessary funds and a fully staffed, highly trained corps of social case workers attached to the schools.

Perhaps if Lincoln had had a visiting counselor with whom the teachers who knew "something was wrong" could have conferred, Charles' later life history might have been different. There are no guarantees that the recognition, referral and treatment of this or any other youth would be successful.

The school teacher has a recognized function: to educate. Time she spends trying to see into her charges' minds and behavior must not be time she owes to the other 25 to 40 students in her class.

Teachers and administrators gave their extra time to Charles, trying to interest him in art, in physical education, in anything. They are not trained case workers who could look at Charles and ask "why" their attempts to reach him failed.

But a trained social worker who could have singled Charles out from the other children who are "just acting up," who would have had time to seek out his parents' cooperation and understanding, and have had the information to refer him to the proper agency or clinic, would be earning a salary around $10,000.

One counselor — even if one could be found — could not handle the entire school system. It is doubtful if such a person could be located to serve in Lincoln. Ask overloaded, under-staffed social agencies who put lack of trained personnel before dollar cost as their biggest problem.

What the Lincoln school system did not do for Charles Starkweather it could not have done with its present facilities. He needed aid and treatment, and so do hundreds of other children not yet "out on their own" — but soon to be.

— Star, Feb. 14, 1958

Starkweather's Dad 'Tired Of Blame'

"I'm tired of taking the blame for this. What could I have done?"

Guy Starkweather, father of the admitted mass murderer Charles Starkweather, is asking the same questions that many Lincolnites have asked themselves.

When Charles quit school at the end of ninth grade, his father had little to say about it. "I wanted Charles to get the schooling I never got," he relates.

"A boy of 16 or 17 has a mind of his own," his father explains. "He was old enough to start making his own decisions."

Charles did make his own decision. He quit school. He started to work full time. He took the step which is considered one of the most important in a teenager's life — the step from "in school" to "on your own."

If Charles had known about the school coordinator of special employment or if that hard-working woman had known about Charles, things might have taken a different turn for the youth at that time.

Her job is to aid in softening the shock of the break with school.

With the aid of a part-time secretary, and job offers from a few (but not enough) Lincoln businessmen, the Lincoln Public Schools coordinator of special employment places an average of 60 teens in half-time supervised employment, and half-time school work.

She "tells them straight" that they are lucky because there are probably 100 other 16-, 15- and 14-year-olds out on their own looking for jobs which are less desirable and harder to find.

She warns them of the rules: neatness, promptness, best work possible at school and job, no "goofing off," no pals dropping in or calling up, and no quitting without telling her first. And she also lends a sympathetic ear, gains the cooperation and understanding of their parents, and, in general, guides without pushing.

Could this school employment counselor have helped Charles? She has helped many teenagers to lose their feelings of insecurity and unimportance. But not all of them responded.

In June, Charles went to work on a full-time basis, serving as a roustabout, moving boxes and bundles, loading trucks. He held the job almost two years, starting at 75 cents an hour on a part-time basis, and earning $1.25 an hour when he quit.

Charles was never a problem, his father relates. He was never a special troublemaker at home, with two older brothers to keep him in line, and a younger sister and two younger brothers to help out with.

"I've tried to figure out every way. What did we do? Mistreat him? No. We were always pretty close. I'd give him extra spending money when he needed it, and he helped us out at home.

"I wish he had come to us when things went wrong, but he didn't. Parents now who interfere are called 'squares,' and the kids, teenagers mostly, seem to run their parents nowadays."

Guy Starkweather remembers that Charles would even do housework, but like most teenagers, "he sort of had to be forced."

Charles wasn't too interested in general repair work, his father's occupation. "He used to come along and help out, and liked working with cement, but never stayed with it," Guy Starkweather recalls.

He liked hunting and was a good shot. He liked cars, fixing them up and tinkering with them. The neighbors sometimes complained because of all the parts and old cars in the backyard of the Starkweather home.

"But there was something he'd work at for hours, and spend all his extra cash on," Mr. Starkweather said.

Once or twice, Mr. Starkweather said, Charles got interested in working around service stations. "He'd hang around and help out and even got to waiting on customers, but sooner or later they'd run him off because he was too young."

Charles once tried to find a job by visiting the Lincoln office of the State Employment Service. He filled out the regular application form with the help of an interviewer.

He met with little success. His age, his lack of job experience, his general appearance, all worked against him. To a trained interviewer, he was easily identified as the hardest type of applicant to place.

If Charles had returned to the employment office, which he did not, about all they could have offered him was "spot" jobs, work assigned each morning to men who appear at the office. The jobs usually last a day or so.

When Charles quit his job at the distributing company, he told his boss he was "getting a job that paid more." It also started at 6 a.m. and ended earlier in the afternoon. Charles had met Caril Fugate and wanted after-school hours free to see her.

He started work as a garbage collector, a job his brother found for him. He wasn't too interested in doing a good job, and resented the "extras" along with the route, which kept him at work after 3 p.m.

Guy Starkweather became worried about his son, and although they never "had words" about it, he felt that "Charlie was being influenced too much by Caril."

He thought Charles was spending his extra pay on the 14-year-old, and knew he was lending his car to her.

"But what could I do?" he questions. "He was old enough to make his own decisions." Mr. Starkweather did talk his son into starting a savings account by asking his employer, the garbage truck owner, to take out "a little each month."

Today, Mr. Starkweather has the account book showing entries of deposits of $15 for October, November and December, from Charles' $42-a-week (after deductions) paycheck.

"He wasn't a bad kid. He tried to do the right things," his father said. "If he had only come to us with his problems."

Child psychologists realize that the gap between parents and child grows wider with every year. By the time a youth reaches adolescence he starts living in a world outside his home. Sometimes a casual observer has more insight into a youth's behavior than his parents do. And the difference between what his parents think he is doing away from home and what he really does is amazing.

The Starkweathers did not know Charles was hanging around a Lincoln pool hall. They did not know of his reputation as a "dare devil" at the Capital Beach auto track where he sometimes drove in "demolition derbies."

They were unaware that he sometimes slept in his car because he had been locked out of his room in a downtown apartment house.

To his parents, Charles talked casually at the breakfast table about the murder of Robert Colvert, a 21-year-old Crest service station attendant. He told them he "wondered" what kind of a guy could have done that and said he thought he'd seen "that guy (Colvert) around town somewhere."

His parents visit Charles at the State Penitentiary now. They talk about what he has done, and ask him what they can do for him.

"I still don't understand," Charles' father admits. "If he had been a problem to us, like some folks say he was, it would have been different. But what could we do?"

— Star, Feb. 15, 1958

If He'd Been A Juvenile Delinquent
Starkweather Might Have Had Help

That kid would have been a hell of a lot better off if he'd been a juvenile delinquent.

This remark, partly in jest, was made by a local law officer. "That kid" is Charles Starkweather.

That kid was not a juvenile delinquent by anyone's definition, legal or clinical. But he admits to mass murder.

What if Charles had had a record as a juvenile law violator? Well, said the officer, if he'd started his "life of crime" with hubcap stealing or maybe vandalism, he'd have been on the records.

If he'd really been in trouble, the police might have "mugged and fingerprinted him." If there had been a record or a picture or descriptions given by people after the first (Colvert) murder, it might have saved a lot of lives.

But how would it have helped Charles to have had "a record"?

The officer went on with his argument. If Charles had been caught at minor crime or even been picked up for being underage in a pool hall or beer tavern, the police, and especially the one juvenile officer assigned to handle all teenage cases for city police, might have talked Charles into going straight, might have ordered him to write a theme on why people should obey the law, might have talked to his folks and warned them about their obligations to keep him out of trouble.

If he had committed a serious offense, or one requiring a payment to an injured party, he would have been sent to the county juvenile authorities for more investigation of the case and perhaps trial in juvenile court.

A talking-to, a non-publicized record, a theme on why to obey the law. That's about all the understaffed office could have offered.

If he'd shown symptoms of mental illness or neglect, a social agency would have received his name and background information. Very few cases are referred, say the social workers. Very few referrals are acted upon, say the police.

In round numbers, about 1,300 juvenile offenders come in contact with the city police every year. Roughly one-third of the cases are handled by the patrol car or beat officer without a visit to the central station. Another third are taken to headquarters for a more thorough investigation. The other third go further and are put into the hands of the county juvenile officers.

A 1955 study made of the handling of juvenile offenders in Lincoln points out the lack of trained personnel at all levels of the city and county juvenile system. One man, with the part-time aid of the two city policewomen, handles a load of cases designed for a department of at least four full-time officers with 24-hour coverage.

But that's no worse than the rest of the city police load where 93 men handle work which, according to surveys of 37 major cities, would require a staff of about 230.

County juvenile personnel are slightly better off. The survey shows that they are (or were in 1955) working at only 200 percent of the ideal capacity. The juvenile probation staff has three full-time workers, plus a secretary. Two graduate students in social work take partial training here. A fully trained staff of nine would be ideal — and costly to the taxpayers. But if there were nine staff members, more space would be required, and have you been in the county courthouse lately?

The juvenile court judgeship rotates among four judges with the district court equity docket.

The assigned juvenile judge also handles divorce proceedings, domestic injunctions, foreclosures, and other odds and ends of equity matters.

This is the situation that a teenager — and by this time his parents, too — meets when he is in relatively "big trouble."

It is not the fault of worker or judge that pre-hearing conferences do not contain all the information and background history necessary by national standards. In fact, it is a major feat of overwork and extra exertion that the juvenile court docket is kept up to date.

The judge works overtime, the case workers and probation officers "make do," the juvenile and his parents get individual (if sometimes hurried) attention, and only the taxpayer comes out ahead. Or does he?

Courts and judges, trained juvenile officers and case workers, adequate space and ideal conference rooms, all cost money. But a jury trial and appeals can cost in the tens of thousands of dollars, and yearly cost of a prisoner in detention ranges around $1,500.

One life sentence would equal quite a few improvements in the juvenile system, in terms of tax money.

Does the prevention of crime and the treatment of the potential criminal cost more than the conviction and detention of the criminal? Surveys nationally point to preventive measures, if adequate, as cheaper. From Lincoln's standpoint it might be "cheaper" than lives and property lost, too.

There is a brighter side to the handling of juvenile delinquency and child neglect cases in Lincoln.

The law, the facilities, the salaries may all be out-moded or inadequate, but the interpretation of the law and the interest of the workers are "extraordinarily fine" in the judgment of outside authorities who recently checked.

Meanwhile, had juvenile authorities in Lincoln had their chance to deal with Charles Starkweather and failed the "why" for his behavior, it would not have been from lack of trying.

The question of what they could have done if they had recognized him as a potential menace or, more likely, a kid in need of treatment, is another problem.

They try for an answer, but they usually come up with more questions. Would one of these officials come up with the right answers to stop Charles Starkweather from becoming a "mad-dog" killer? Or would he have been filed away as an unsolved problem?

— Star, Feb. 17, 1958

**Starkweather Case Points Up Problem
Of How To Identify Needs, Meet Them**

"What could I have done to prevent this?"

Again and again in conversation, Lincolnites who had direct contact with Charles Starkweather ask this question.

The answer they expect is: "Nothing."

To fail to identify those in need of help is to be responsible for their neglect and future problems.

To miss the signs of maladjustment or neglect in Charles Starkweather or in any other persons is not only possible but probable, but to recognize these signs and to disregard them is the fault of the individual and the community.

Some of the people who asked this question had taken the obvious step — to speak to the parents. No, they did not say "your son is maladjusted" or "you must curb his anti-social tendencies."

Instead, they spoke of Charles' inability to "get along" or of his disinterest in subjects or activities.

One adult, who had been worried about Charles' behavior in his Sunday School class, went to the Starkweathers with his problem. When he arrived, he admitted he could bring himself to speak only of Charles' irregular attendance record and to add a plea that the parents set a better example for their son.

Yes, Charles attended Sunday School. From 1944 to 1954, he attended Sunday School classes 122 times in the church where he was baptized. Then he was dropped from the roster because of his poor attendance record, which averaged about four Sundays a year during the later years.

Despite the efforts of a close relative and repeated attempts of the church pastor and church workers, Charles left the church about the same time he left school, and lost another contact with the community which knew so little about him.

There must be an answer for that Sunday School teacher who attempted and failed to voice his concern and interest in Charles.

At present, there is no single answer to give the adult who believes he must seek aid other than the parents about the behavior of a child. Personal reasons aside, perhaps some case workers could have explained the situation to the family much more fully than the church worker.

A trained social worker, a juvenile officer or a school authority are all possible sources of aid to the problem which that adult faced.

Lincoln has more than 65 social, health, welfare and aid organizations, each performing a specific function in meeting community needs. Some deal with individuals, some with special age groups, some with families. Bylaws and constitutions outline their functions and methods but do not tell the entire story.

One of these agencies, and more probably several of them, might have helped the outsider who had information on a family problem.

How to find the correct agency is another matter. Even the organizations themselves are not aware of all the services offered by the others. The Lincoln Community Council, formerly the Council of Social Agencies, is one contact to the various groups. Although its personnel do not have all the answers, they are likely to know those who might help.

The problem of the perplexed church worker brings out several factors in the picture of community services and governmental agencies handling community problems in Lincoln.

Why is there no liaison organization where a trained worker could handle the quandary of this well-intentioned person?

Social welfare workers are the first to admit that there are many deficiencies in their present functioning.

To name a few: lack of trained workers in almost every field, including recreation, psychiatric aid, counseling, health; lack of funds to hire adequate staff to handle case loads and to pay adequate salaries to attract and keep their best-qualified and most permanent personnel; lack of a guiding hand to integrate efforts to expand and to remedy situations of duplication and inefficiency; little time or interest to consider the use of other groups' facilities; and lack of information available to the public about their organizations.

A family seeking financial aid might go to a welfare agency. After investigation, the family might or might not receive aid to feed and clothe them until they get "over the hump" and "back on their feet again."

The welfare agency investigation might also have turned up the need for mental or physical treatment, vocational rehabilitation, solution of marital problems or correction of unhealthy home situations.

The subsistence level at which welfare agencies must allot their funds does not allow for coverage of such "by-products" or side issues directly.

The lack of "integration" — a big word for "working together" — among specialized groups becomes apparent. The agency contacted handles the case with its own resources. To request outside aid from other agencies is considered, in most cases, a poor policy.

Referrals from one agency to another do occur. Police, schools, courts all have systems for summoning aid from agencies. Direct referral from one agency to another is less frequent, partly because of the overloads all carry. Direct referral could turn into a "pass-the-buck" system, social workers themselves feel.

If unmet needs are uncovered by one agency, the individual receiving aid may be informed of the other sources of aid and the need for contacting other organizations. But the "reaching out" for additional help must again come from the person or family with a problem.

Nationally and locally, there is recognition that welfare and service agencies of a community are about 30 years outdated. Horse-and-buggy methods to meet atomic-age problems are constantly cited by writers in the field.

Facts on juvenile delinquency show the problem that every agency, not just those dealing with youthful offenders, must meet by 1975. If the present juvenile delinquency rate (1.5 percent of the nation's juveniles now come in contact with the courts) and the population increase rate both remain constant, the courts will be faced with about 60 percent more juvenile cases than they must handle now.

It is unnecessary to add that juvenile delinquency rates are not remaining constant but increasing. Authorities in all social welfare fields view the increase in case loads plus the population growth with well-founded alarm.

"Viewing with alarm" is an unfair comment on what individual agencies, and their coordinating group, are doing about the present lack of cooperation in meeting the problems in Lincoln.

The present focus of attention placed on Lincoln's public service agencies is one which, under different circumstances, they would welcome.

As one director put it: Charles Starkweather may accomplish something which would have taken many years of halting progress to achieve — the awakening of the social welfare groups themselves to their need for each other.

At present, three Lincoln groups are working toward establishment of full-time psychiatric service in Lincoln. Why three groups? Why not one coordinated study and plan?

The need for a united effort in meeting both immediate lacks and long-range needs of the community service programs was recognized long before the Charles Starkweather case.

Outsiders have viewed the system, talked to workers and returned to their respective homes to prepare reports and recommendations.

Some of these recommendations are predictable by the Lincoln groups surveyed. Among them may well be plans for:

— A stronger central clearing house, to act as coordinator of effort, to initiate united action where the need appears the greatest.

— Closer work with schools, law enforcement and juvenile officers and with other agencies, plus a better system of utilizing special services offered by the federal and state governments, the University of Nebraska, and other Nebraska institutions.

— A better "referral" system and central information agency where families and individuals in need of help will be referred to the agency best able to handle the situation.

— Changes in the scope and coverage of some groups to remove present overlapping functions and allow more intensified work in a well-defined field.

— Star, Feb. 19, 1958

Starkweather Case 'Big City' Problem

"I wanted to be somebody, be important — but not this important."

Charles Starkweather is reported to have said this to a Wyoming deputy sheriff after his capture.

A local sociologist comments wryly that Charles did more in making Lincoln important than Lincoln ever did for Charles.

Lincolnites seem, in their own conversations about the Starkweather case, to have recognized other symptoms which prove to them the premise that Lincoln is no longer a "small town" where we get together and talk things out, where everyone is known by name or occupation and where everyone is recognized as a member — a part — of the community.

Lincoln now lacks something that a smaller community has — a sense of belonging, a sense of being recognized, accepted or disapproved.

The "other symptoms" of Lincoln's growth into a big city, which have shown up in the past year as teenage statistics, include three suicides of Lincoln area teenagers, a knife attack upon an elderly woman by a youth, and a beating with a baseball bat by another youngster.

What is wrong with a society in which young people feel they must take a life — their own or another?

Monday in another state a 33-year-old Lincolnite, who began his criminal record at the age of 11 by vandalism at Lincoln's Cotner

College, will face charges on three counts of armed robbery, and auto theft, rape and operation of a motor vehicle without the owner's consent. His life span between these two ages is marked by charges and sentences involving burglary, robbery, rape, assault, larceny and escape.

Big city and crime are not synonymous, but crime is expected and not questioned in a larger city. From the reactions which the Starkweather case produced in Lincoln, the citizens have proved they have not yet developed the callous attitude required to dismiss the tragedy of mass killing or the lessons taught by an "unimportant" teenager who admits to murder.

No one — or at least a very small minority of Lincolnites — wishes to return to the "good old days" when kids played kids' tricks, and both father and son shared the cold stares of the town because Junior yanked the trolley boom off the electric cable.

Lincoln has grown up but still prides itself in being young, and still expects its citizens to live by the rules of "responsibility to the community" when the community has abandoned its responsibility to the individual.

The police force, welfare agencies, courts, schools and churches now have taken over the functions of discipline, aid and attention to the individual which once the community as a whole performed.

The charity Christmas baskets have been replaced by investigation and aid (not charity); the cold stares and personal attention of the community have been given over to the police and social workers, the Boy Scouts and the juvenile courts.

In surrendering its responsibilities to specialized agencies, the community has lost its direct approach and, therefore, part of its effectiveness in controlling the behavior of the individual.

The "reaching out" which Lincoln once accomplished by personal attention to every citizen has become a "make an appointment and we'll be glad to look into this" approach to the teenager, the family and the neighborhood.

One theorist suggests that the cost of the trials of Charles and Caril, plus the loss of lives and other expensive side issues, would have paid for "years and years" of preventive methods and adequate facilities for youth.

What are some of the needs of Lincoln as outlined by the school, social welfare, judicial and enforcement authorities?

— A juvenile court judge on a full-time basis with an adequate and trained staff.

— A system of "early detection" in the schools to spot the pre-delinquent or maladjusted child, and a later program of counseling and guidance before the ending of formal education.

— A coordinated and fully staffed social welfare program encompassing all agencies and furnishing a liaison with other outside sources.

— A full-time mental health clinic, adequately staffed.

— A law enforcement system, city and county, which includes a special division to handle juvenile offenders.

But planning the "ideal" system is not the only problem. To get the job done requires immediate action on a "first things first" basis, a coordination of existing facilities for better efficiency.

The setting up of systems is not enough, one youth worker points out. Those systems must be used. Community interest, community surveillance and community funds are needed.

The critical view of an outsider is expressed in his opinion that Lincoln has the needed facilities but not the needed coordination and none of the needed outside interest.

Noted lawyer and mystery writer Erle Stanley Gardner commented recently that "if the average community had half as much interest in its police as the police have in the community, we would have far less crime." He might have included community systems of education and aid in this statement.

Gardner added that "the next big development in law enforcement must come from the people rather than the police."

The directors and workers in all fields of social welfare and protection are aware and are acting on the premise that the people of Lincoln are concerned about the present system which allows such teenagers as Charles Starkweather to spend 19 years in the community without a single hand "reaching out" with aid or guidance.

The community may expect the launching of many pilot projects and expansion or coordination plans from these agencies in the near future. If these plans become a reality, they must give part of the credit to Charles Starkweather.

— *Star, Feb. 20, 1958*

Comments Highlight Case

The opinion of the individual Lincolnite has been the source of most of the information in this series. It seems only fair, therefore, to include some comments and questions which have come from these interested persons, but have not been included in the series.

1. To the parents of the teenagers who knew Charles and rejected him: Authorities point out that a child's peers are the best judges of his character. Any guilt these teenagers feel is shared by the community which failed to recognize their opinions as potential danger signals.

2. To the questioners who ask why the guilt of 11 killings is being "whitewashed" and the blame placed on the community: The purpose of gathering the opinions of authorities was not to whitewash Charles Starkweather, but to alert the community to the needs of youth not now being met. An impartial jury will determine

Charles' future.

3. To the Lincolnites who have asked why Charles Starkweather was not drafted "and given some sort of respect for authority": The local selective service office operates on a strict policy of age and classification. At present, potential draftees are classified at about 21 and, if found eligible for the draft, inducted at about 22. A side comment is: The Army is not a correctional institution or a place to send youths who are a potential threat to their home-towns.

4. To every citizen who feels he or she shares the blame for Charles Starkweathers's actions, a comment from another citizen: Let's quit blaming ourselves and each other for this crime and fix the responsibility on all of us for the next one. There will be a "next one" if we don't start thinking constructively — and perhaps even if we do.

5. To those persons who wish to place the major portion of the blame for the Starkweather case upon the inadequacy of the Lincoln and Lancaster County law enforcement agencies: Disregarding any opinions citizens may have on the adequacy or inadequacy of the investigation and attempted capture of the teenagers, the facts remain that the budgets and personnel of these law enforcement agencies are geared to the normal routine they are expected to meet. The ability to catch a criminal lies in the training, the numbers and the attitudes of law officers. The taxpayers and voters are the ultimate judges of these factors, not the patrolman on the beat.

6. To the Lincolnites who have expressed concern that the youth recreation program of the city did not reach this youth: Sports and games do not cure delinquency, experts say. The busy youth may be the non-delinquent youth, but the youth programs of the city are voluntary activities not designed to seek out the maladjusted or neglected child. The fact that this youth and others are not attracted by group youth activities is one factor that is being studied in planning youth programs of the future.

7. To the adult who places the blame for youth crime upon comic books and television: Then why do the 98.5 percent of teenagers without juvenile records not fall under these same influences?

8. To those who believe Charles could have killed all the people he wanted without arousing the community if he had not selected one wealthy family: Charles Starkweather did not pick his victims for publicity. If he had, he could not have done a better job. He struck at north Lincoln, south Lincoln and nearby rural Bennet, bringing the meaning of death very close to the entire area.

— Star, Feb. 20, 1958

In the 35 years since 1958, there have been substantial improvements in services by schools and social agencies for young people who have difficulties. But journalists do not recall that those improvements came as an immediate reaction to the Starkweather case.

Fugate, 15, was sent to the Women's Reformatory at York for a life term.

Freedom, but not exoneration

Caril Fugate was found guilty in the death of Robert Jensen, 17, of Bennet on Friday, Nov. 21, 1958, and was sentenced to life in prison, but under Nebraska law and rules it was anticipated that she might be free by age 31. She was taken to the state Women's Reformatory at York, where she settled in as an inmate, separated from other prisoners by a state law requiring that those under 16 be segregated from the general population.

At York, her routine included three hours a week of instruction by an institution teacher.

When Caril became ill a month later, she was admitted to the York General Hospital under a false name and kept there for two and a half days without any guards. Her treatment was far different from that given to Charles Starkweather at the state Penitentiary.

There were a number of legal skirmishes surrounding the eventual execution of Starkweather on June 24, 1959. Caril's attorney sought a stay to permit additional questioning of Starkweather, based on a contontion that the condemned murderer had been influenced to testify against his girlfriend. The stay was not granted.

Told of Starkweather's execution, Caril Fugate "felt sorry for him, but she wasn't moved or anything like that," according to her attorney. "The first thing she asked me after I told her of the execution was, 'Did he tell the truth before he died?' " the attorney reported.

Nearing her 16th birthday on July 30, 1959, Carol Fugate was reported doing well in her schoolwork at the reformatory. She passed eighth-grade requirements and started taking courses through the University of Nebraska's correspondence high school.

The legal appeals of her conviction began on Nov. 30, 1958, nine days after sentencing, when her attorney asked for a new trial and alleged 71 errors in the trial proceedings. That request was denied on Dec. 20, but the ruling was appealed at the end of January to the Nebraska Supreme Court. The high court quickly turned down a request to suspend sentence while the appeal proceeded, and it eventually denied the appeal. That action in turn was taken to the U.S. Supreme Court, where it again was denied. A second appeal, based on a bet by a Fugate juror before jurors were chosen, also was turned down quickly.

On July 9, 1964, attorneys asked the U.S. District Court in Lincoln for a writ of habeas corpus. The court denied the request. Later that year the federal court did rule that a new Supreme Court decision on availability of counsel should apply in the Fugate case, and the U.S. Court of Appeals returned the case to the state courts for determination of whether the girl's rights had been violated. The state courts denied they had.

Another retrial bid through the federal courts came in 1970-1972, ending with denial by the U.S. Supreme Court on Oct. 11, 1972.

Other landmark events in Caril Fugate's life were noted occasionally in the press, such as this story just before her 21st birthday by Nancy Ray (who, as Nancy Benjamin, had covered the girl's trial):

Caril, Nearing 21, Eager For Freedom, Nursing Career

At 21, a girl traditionally becomes a woman. She plans for marriage, a home, children, a career, travel, adventure, with the belief that the whole world is at her feet.

For Caril Ann Fugate, who celebrates her 21st birthday Thursday, all such thoughts end at the front gate of the Reformatory for Women.

"I can't plan beyond that," says the intense, dark-haired girl. "First, I must get out."

For over 5½ years, Caril has been in the women's prison in York serving a life sentence for first degree murder in connection with the mass murder spree of Charles Starkweather, since executed.

Is she guilty of an active part in that world-famous string of homicides? Caril answers in a toneless voice. "Maybe if I say it again and again, a thousand and a thousand more times that I didn't do anything, that I am not guilty, people will believe me. Sometimes people say that they believe me, but I can tell — in their faces, in their eyes, I guess — that they really don't."

Does she still think and dream about the horrors of those January days in 1958 when she was witness to the deaths of family and strangers? "No, I closed the door on that. I have never had any nightmares about it. And I try not to think or talk about it."

About the publicity and trial, Caril still shows emotion which she explains is caused because: "I should have had a chance to tell my side. I should have had my say. People just don't realize what fear can do."

Caril adds that she has "no hard feelings" about her treatment,

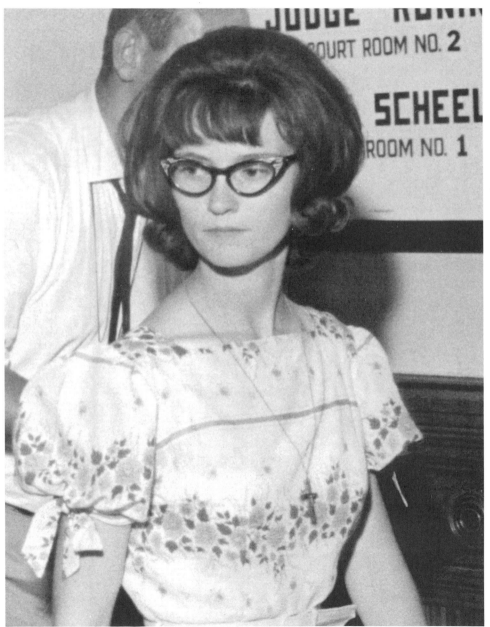

Fugate was denied bond pending a post-conviction appeal in 1965.

and says that she plans to write a book "about the whole thing" when she gets out of prison.

When will she get out? "I don't know, but I have hope," says Caril. At present a habeas corpus action in her behalf is pending in Federal District Court which, if successful, could grant Caril her freedom long before the average parole time of 30 years.

If and when she gets out, Caril says, her goal is to become a nurse. Why a nurse? "I'd like to do something where I was helping people. I think I'd be a pretty good nurse and I plan to take a nursing course here after I finish high school," Caril explained.

Would she change her name when she got out? "I've thought about it a lot. It would be the easiest way, but it would be running away, and you can't run away from anything. And I think why should I change my name? I haven't done anything."

Would she ever consider getting married? "I'm not sure. I've been burnt once, and I'd certainly take a long, long time about it and be sure I was doing the right thing."

The girl who gave this interview a week before her 21st birthday looks far different from the panicked 14-year-old captured with Starkweather in January 1958. She was then a dirty, tired, pouting teenager whose eyes darted glances of hate and distrust at those around her.

Today, Caril looks younger and acts much more mature. She is a short 5-1 in height which allows just the toes of her sneaker-clad feet to touch in a lounge chair in the superintendent's office. She weighs less than 100 lbs., has a trim size 9 figure.

Her nails, her hair, her skin, her smile bespeak much interest in her personal appearance not always found in women's institutions.

Her voice is steady, her answers direct, her smile much in evidence. Her manner is reserved with strangers but not from shyness, snobbishness or design. Perhaps Caril finds it hard to trust a stranger, not an uncommon trait.

Superintendent Gladys Ellenson, who acknowledges she considers Caril "a fine young woman," notes her good conduct at the institution during the nearly five years Mrs. Ellenson has been there.

Mrs. Ellenson and her husband live at the institution and sometimes invite Caril to their quarters to watch TV on their color set. (Her favorite program: "Bonanza.")

The superintendent attests to Caril's poise and maturity, and to her will to accomplish what goals she sets herself. Mrs. Ellenson is proud of the development of this child into a woman under the regimen of work and discipline at the prison.

And Caril believes she is ready now to face her future in the free world. The next question to be answered is whether the free world is ready to accept Caril Fugate.

— *Star, July 27, 1964*

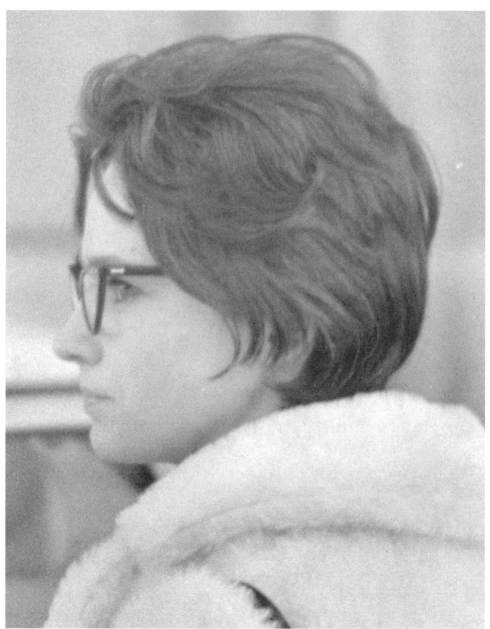

In 1970, Fugate tried — but failed — to win a retrial bid in the federal courts.

From the time of her imprisonment, Caril Fugate's case was reviewed annually by the Nebraska Parole Board, which had the power to recommend that the state Pardon Board commute her sentence to a definite period of years, which eventually would lead to her release.

Marj Marlette, writing in August 1972 that the upcoming Fugate case would be a most difficult one for parole and pardon officials, noted:

> She has grown up in prison. She has finished high school, become an expert seamstress, a knowledgeable tour guide and sort of a senior inmate counselor at the small institution. She knows not only the rules and programs of the prison, but also the reasons for them.
>
> She helps in the nursery of a York church on Sundays, has earned the privileges of going bowling, occasionally shopping, and swimming in town. (This summer, she learned to swim, although it took her a month to get over her fear of the water, she explains.)
>
> — *Journal, Aug. 20, 1972*

In June 1973, Nebraska's Parole Board set an Aug. 22 hearing in the case. At that hearing, the board voted to ask the Pardon Board to commute her sentence.

Caril Fugate was reported in The Star as "thrilled and deeply touched by efforts on her behalf." The superintendent of the reformatory said the young woman "believes it was the hand of God that directed and guided the decision."

During the hearing, a number of witnesses testified for her:

33 Witnesses Back Caril Fugate's Freedom Bid

Her case bolstered by supporting testimony from 33 witnesses, including the state's corrections director, Caril Ann Fugate Wednesday took her bid for freedom to the state Board of Paroles.

Dressed in white, Miss Fugate, now a composed woman of 30 who has lived more than half of her life in prison, told the board's three members that her efforts to gain freedom in the courts have been exhausted.

"I pursued my case in the courts until the last door was closed," she said.

"If the purpose of an institution is to rehabilitate," she said, "I feel the institution has done as much as it can."

Miss Fugate sat directly across a table from the board members to plead her case in a hearing at the state Penitentiary.

Chairman John Greenholtz said the board will announce Friday whether it will approve a request to present to the Board of Pardons her appeal for commutation of her life sentence for murder to a definite term of years, thereby making her eligible for conditional parole by the Board of Paroles.

Fugate became a talented seamstress during her years at the reformatory.

The outlook for that initial approval appeared favorable.

"She stood up real well under our questions," Greenholtz told newsmen after the three-hour hearing.

Repeating a phrase he had used twice before during the hearing, the former prison offcial suggested: "To know Caril is to like her.

"She impressed me, as she always has, as to her sincerity."

Five persons — including four relatives of two of the victims — testified against Miss Fugate's plea.

Mrs. Robert Jensen of Bennet, mother of Bob Jensen, killed at age 17, read in a trembling voice a handwritten statement suggesting that 15 years of imprisonment is not punishment which fits the crime.

"It isn't long enough for any of us," Mrs. Mabel King Swale, the mother of Carol King, a teenager who died with Jensen, told the board.

"I think she should stay there (in York)."

Miss Fugate left the hearing before any witnesses were escorted into the board room.

Testifiying in her behalf were the pastor and 20 members of the Church of the Nazarene in York, where Miss Fugate works in the nursery during church services; a Michigan couple who learned of her case when they saw a network television documentary, and a former fellow inmate at York, who was accompanied by her mother.

State Corrections Director Vic Walker urged the board to "give serious consideration" to Miss Fugate's request.

"You won't find a woman (prisoner) in the U.S. who has made the cooperative effort that this girl has," Walker said. "She has responded to every opportunity.

"If anyone, by their behavior and cooperation, has earned consideration, Caril has. We're not capable of giving her any more help at this time."

Earlier, Miss Fugate had told the board that she decided when she entered the institution at age 15 (she was 14 when she accompanied Starkweather on the rampage) to "take advantage of . . . whatever they had to offer."

— Star, Aug. 23, 1973

Then on Oct. 31 came the action of the Pardon Board:

Pardon Board Makes Caril Fugate Eligible For Parole

Caril Ann Fugate, who as a 14-year-old accompanied Charles Starkweather on a 1958 murder spree through Nebraska and Wyoming, will be eligible for parole in June 1976.

The State Pardon Board on a 2-1 vote Tuesday commuted the 30-year-old Miss Fugate's life sentence for first degree murder to no less than 30 years or more than 50 years imprisonment. Gov. J. James Exon and Secretary of State Allen Beermann favored the commutation with Attorney General Clarence A.H. Meyer casting the dissent.

The action opens the way for Miss Fugate to come before the five-man Parole Board in May 1976, for a review of possible parole. However, if future Parole Boards oppose Miss Fugate's release, her parole could be delayed until September 1987, under the terms of the commutation.

— Star, Oct. 31, 1973

In 1973, the Starkweather murder spree was the "take-off point" for a film, "Badlands," which The New York Times critic found "blunt and beautiful." Caril Fugate saw the film, but had no comment.

In September 1974, she finished training and passed her exams with excellent grades for certification as a geriatrics nurse aide.

In 1973, Fugate won commutation of her life sentence.

In June 1975, her final hearing before the Parole Board was set for June 20, 1976. At that time she would be eligible for parole. The board actually met June 8, and acted after hearing no opposition. Marj Marlette wrote the story for the Journal:

Caril Ann Fugate Granted Parole

YORK — A beaming Caril Ann Fugate got parole Tuesday.

And if she has her announced way, it will be the last time the lights go on, the cameras flash, and tapes and pencils record her words.

She had asked for no more publicity.

The decision to parole Miss Fugate was made on a 4-1 vote, Parole Board Chairman John Greenholtz said. In favor were Greenholtz, Eugene Neal, Ed Rowley, all of Lincoln, and Marshall Tate, Omaha. Catherine Dahlquist, Omaha, cast the only negative vote.

Greenholtz said Miss Fugate would go out of state under interstate parole compact. He said she would report to a parole officer in Michigan.

Her parole agreement, a standard form, includes observing the laws, staying away from undesirable companions, maintaining employment and residence, and not owning firearms or harmful narcotics.

There was, in an unexpected development, no opposition to Miss Fugate at the hearing held in a new building at the Nebraska Center for Women.

Letters were received opposed to her release, but not a single person appeared to testify against her.

Previously, any hearings on clemency for Miss Fugate — Charles Starkweather's companion in a murder spree that left 10 dead, 18 years ago — had attracted considerable opposition.

Tuesday, the petite Miss Fugate, her curly brown hair shining and shoulder length, her white dress tailored and trim — had a question for the board.

"Being in the position I'm in, what kind of action could I possibly take in the future to eliminate the publicity I want to avoid?

"I simply want to go out and do the best I can. I do not want any publicity."

Board members told her it wouldn't be easy, but "you have a right to live as a private citizen." They said, too, they had been concerned about the possibility of her being exploited.

It was agreed to make a stipulation in her parole agreement that she would hold no press conferences and grant no interviews without the specific written permission of the Parole Board and the Michigan agency supervising her.

Caril assured the board her plea was sincere. "I'm not saying one thing to get out, then flaunt it and do another thing."

In a hearing before the state Parole Board in 1976, Fugate won her freedom.

Miss Fugate, who has been at the women's prison since she was 15, said she hoped to get married and have a couple of kids — "just be a regular little dumpy old housewife."

Asked what she had learned in prison, she said, "I think I've learned to say no. I think, too, I've learned compassion."

Of the "people who have hated me for 18 years," she said she felt sorry. "It has destroyed their lives."

Among five witnesses on her behalf, Shelly Pesek, a correctional officer at the women's center until three weeks ago, said she had worked closely with Caril, "and I feel she's such a warm person. . . ."

Pamela Epp, director of the Henderson Nursing Home, where Caril has been on work release for two and a half years, said, "Caril has demonstrated she could take on responsibility. . . . We've learned to love her as a person."

She said the young woman had learned to handle frustration as time went by.

Paul Kirst, administrator of the nursing home, said "she has developed tremendously in her ability." He mentioned particularly her ability to communicate with the staff.

— Journal, June 8, 1976

And in the next day's paper:

For Caril, Michigan Is Hope

YORK — From a small prison in Nebraska to an unidentified small town in Michigan, Caril Ann Fugate's life soon will take a major change.

She will be free under parole supervision.

After 18 years in the Nebraska Center for Women (formerly the women's reformatory), she will get a chance to become "just a regular old dumpy housewife" and fade from the headlines and the television tubes.

She will live with a young couple she has had contact with for some time.

She will work in that family's business.

Someday, she hopes, she will marry and have children.

Originally, Miss Fugate, now 32, was sentenced to life for first-degree murder in the 1958 death of Robert Jensen, 17, of Bennet. This was commuted to a 30- to 50-year term in 1973 by the state Board of Pardons.

For the same crime — one in a series of 10 murders — Charles Starkweather went to the electric chair.

The 30-year minimum made Miss Fugate eligible for parole June 20, the date she will be released. She will report to a parole officer in St. John's, Mich.

She must live up to certain standard parole provisions — observe all laws, maintain employment and residence and stay away from undesirable companions — or she can be returned to serve up to the 50-year maximum.

An additional stipulation in her case, that she not hold press conferences or grant interviews without Nebraska Parole Board and Michigan parole authority permission, was added after she expressed a desire to avoid publicity.

None of the provisions should cause her any problems, she told the parole board at her hearing Tuesday.

Miss Fugate will be on parole until Sept. 4, 1987, according to parole board computations. This date was arrived at by taking her maximum term less time off credited for institutional and parole good behavior. The parole board could discharge her from parole at an earlier date, but it is unlikely.

At the Women's Center, meanwhile, Supt. Jacqueline Crawford said she and other staff members were delighted with Miss Fugate's parole. She said Miss Fugate had earned it. She also said, "Michigan suggested that perhaps she (Caril) should change her name. We discussed that and I discussed it with Caril."

Mrs. Crawford said a name change "is a possibility, but it is something that would be done if incidents make it necessary."

— *Journal, June 9, 1976*

Less than two weeks later came a wire story from St. Johns:

Town Accepts Fugate

ST. JOHNS, MICH. — This quiet mid-Michigan farming community has accepted without question — almost without a thought — the anonymous presence of parolee Caril Ann Fugate.

City officials said Monday they knew little about the 32-year-old woman released from a Nebraska prison during the weekend after serving 18 years on a first degree murder conviction.

State corrections officials who knew her whereabouts declined to discuss the case, refusing even to confirm that she had arrived in Michigan.

"Caril Fugate would like to be as anonymous as possible," said corrections department spokesman Gail Light. "Our main concern is for her."

It was a 1972 television special called "Growing Up in Prison" that brought a St. Johns-area couple to the aid of Miss Fugate, according to Jackie Crawford, warden at the Women's Reformatory in York, Neb., where Miss Fugate had been serving a life term for murder.

"These are beautiful people," said Mrs. Crawford of the Michigan couple who offered Miss Fugate a home and "responsible" clerical job in a business they own near St. Johns.

"They saw the TV special, came to the prison to meet her and they became friends. Now they are going to help her get a new start on life."

— *Journal, June 22, 1976*

A year later, Caril Fugate was reported doing very well in the Michigan town. After another year came a story that she had asked permission of the Nebraska Parole Board to marry but that the marriage had been postponed by mutual consent.

It was five years later that Caril Fugate's ultimate freedom came:

Parole Discharge Makes Caril Ann Fugate A Free Woman

Caril Ann Fugate did what she said she'd do when she left the Nebraska Center for Women five years ago: She became a private citizen, refused interviews and media coverage and did her parole without fanfare.

She has worked in a hospital, minded her own business and earned the praise of those supervising her parole.

Now, at 38, she's free to go where she wants.

Ms. Fugate, the teen-age companion of Charles Starkweather in a series of murders that terrorized Lincoln and Lancaster County 23 years ago, has been discharged from her parole by the Nebraska Board of Parole.

"The usual procedure is to consider a lifer for discharge after five years on parole, unless there's some special reason not to," Board Chairman John Greenholtz explained Monday. Her parole officer had recommended a discharge for several years, Greenholtz said.

Without a discharge, she would have been on parole until 1987.

There never had been any problems reported with Ms. Fugate's parole in Michigan, where she was supervised through an interstate parole compact, said Greenholtz and Nebraska Parole Administrator Larry Tewes.

Her attitude was positive, she remained employed and she had no contact with law enforcement since her release, Tewes said.

She has not married, although at least twice she reportedly was considering it, Greenholtz confirmed.

She has lived a quiet life working as an orderly or nurse's aide in a Michigan hospital.

Lucille Splinter, assistant superintendent at the Center for Women and one of the people who knew Ms. Fugate well, said that "Caril broke all ties" when she left Nebraska, but Mrs. Splinter had contacted her for a while afterward.

"I think she came through a caring, thinking person," Mrs. Splinter said. "She wasn't a vegetable. She has a temper, has emotion. What would we be like, locked up 18 years?"

"I think she had some disappointments in the free world," the assistant superintendent continued, but "you have to admire her. When she left, she said she didn't want any publicity, and she stuck to it."

At her parole hearing, she asked the board to stipulate that she wasn't to give interviews or have contact with the media without the board's permission. They agreed.

She never asked for that permission.

— Journal, Sept. 28, 1981

Caril Fugate's opposition to publicity soon evaporated, however, apparently because of renewed desire on her part to win public acceptance of her claim of innocence.

In 1983 she appeared on the television series "Lie Detector." At a press conference the day she recorded her appearance, she said she would be "satisfied" with an apology from Nebraskans, and she continued her long contention that she had been forced to go along with Starkweather on his murder spree.

On the show, noted trial lawyer F. Lee Bailey concluded that lie detector tests showed that 14-year-old Caril Fugate was unaware her parents already had been murdered when she went with Starkweather in January 1958, and that she believed she needed to go with Starkweather to protect members of her family.

The TV show stirred up a flurry of public controversy, including a poll that indicated fewer than half of Nebraskans believed her story.

In 1986, the Starkweather affair was the subject of a documentary by Omaha television station WOW-T. Station staff members interviewed Caril Fugate extensively, but she declined to be quoted on the show.

Journal-Star newspaper files include only a scattering of stories about Caril Fugate after that, but there is this 1990 entry:

Fugate Mails Testimony From Mass-Murder Trial

Authorities said Thursday that Caril Ann Fugate has mailed about 200 copies of testimony from the Starkweather-Fugate mass murder trial to Lincoln-area residents since early August.

In a telephone conversation between Fugate and Sgt. Noah Van Butsel Thursday, Fugate said she mailed the testimonies "so that the people of Nebraska would know" that her "first confession was the true confession," Van Butsel said.

Fugate served 18 years of a life sentence in connection with the killing of a 17-year-old Bennet man. She and her former boyfriend, Charles Starkweather, were taken into custody in Wyoming in early 1958.

She has maintained that Starkweather forced her to accompany him on a rampage that left 10 people dead, three of whom were Fugate's father, mother and sister. Fugate has said she did not learn of her family members' deaths until her capture in Wyoming.

Van Butsel said Fugate told him the recipients of the mailings were selected randomly. He said the copies that have been turned in to police are similar in content. Most of the envelopes were postmarked Flint, Mich., or Lansing, Mich.

Linda Nolte of 7330 Knox Court said a copy of the testimonies was delivered to her residence Tuesday. Nolte said Caril Fugate's name was rubber stamped in ink on the outside of the envelope.

She said most of the testimony was that of Starkweather and detailed how he killed Fugate's family at their Lincoln home.

The few pages of transcript devoted to Fugate's testimony indicated that Fugate was not present during the murders, Nolte said.

Nolte said Fugate's affirmative response to the question if she had been in school at the time of the murders was circled.

Fugate was paroled in 1978 and moved to Michigan. She was released from parole in September 1981.

— Star, Sept. 14, 1990

· Since those letters mailed in 1990, there has been only silence from Caril Fugate — now a woman of 50. Reports in early 1993 about the filming of a television miniseries, "Starkweather: Murder in the Heartland," drew no public reaction from her.

Questions about her role in the 1958 murder spree remain essentially unanswered.

ABOUT THE AUTHOR

Earl Dyer is a native Nebraskan and a graduate of the University of Nebraska. He joined the staff of The Lincoln Star while still a student at the university. He became city editor in 1951 and was named executive editor in 1960, serving at that post until his retirement in April 1992. In those positions he handled a number of major stories, but none that were bigger for The Lincoln Star than the Starkweather case. On the day the first bodies were found, Lincoln Star managing editor Larry Becker was out of town on vacation; the 30-year-old Dyer was thrown in charge of the paper's coverage. He remembers working more than 70 hours that week.

Legacy of Images.

A captivating look at forty years of photojournalism.

Over the past four decades, photographers from the Lincoln Journal-Star
have captured thousands of images on film.
Everything from blizzards to Big Red, Farm Aid to ferocious fires, Nixon to Starkweather.
All of the important events that make up the history of Lincoln and Nebraska.

Filled with over 100 pages of photographs,
Legacy of Images is a keepsake for anyone who loves history and enjoys great photography.

Order yours today while quantities last.

To order, complete and mail
the order form below, with payment, to:
Legacy of Images
c/o Lincoln Journal-Star
926 P Street
Lincoln, NE 68508

O R D E R   F O R M

NAME _____

ADDRESS_____

CITY _____STATE_____ZIP_____

copies ordered _____ x $15.95 =   _____
Shipping & handling (per book - via UPS)   2.95
Subtotal   _____
6.5 % Sales Tax   _____
(outside of Lincoln, add appropriate local sales tax)
TOTAL $_____

Legacy of Images
Four decades of Lincoln Journal-Star photojournalism